DEDICATION

To aiming high, stopping to smell the flowers, and sharing the gifts of life with loved ones and others we meet along the way.

Dedicated to my better half Beth Darnell; my brother, daughter, and son; all our wonderful family members and friends; and to all the illustrious clients of The Darnell Works Agency, past and present.

I also wish to thank some of the many people who have reshaped my world through their kindness, support, and generosity. In addition to those already named, I am also eternally grateful to Leslie "Jinx" Caulfield, Alice Wright, Susana Crofton, Mike Sullivan, Giles Hoglin, Keith Fowles, Bob Davis, R. Scott Horner, Eric Dentel, Gay Henderson, Jay Lerew, Randy Baker, Pamela Tuscany, Arthur Gross, Bruce Merwin, Dwayne Shattuck, Mathew Hayden, Hardy Edwards, Bob Storer, Zoe Iltsopoulos Borys, Connie Swanson, Mitch Mentor, Billy Mead, Gina Schifano, Boris Malden, Steve Beers, Leslie Stevens, Patrick Hasburgh, Clifton Campbell, Michael Ironside, Kacy Palmieri, Mike Vu, Dick Wilson, John Melfi, Graham Yost, Tom Hanks, Amy McKenzie, Christopher Cowen, John Walker, Ron Stein, Tim Street, Ted Schilowitz, Lisa Cleff-Kurtz, Mike Garfinkel, Michael Terpin, Will Travis, Ric Peralta, Simon Needham, Angus Wall, Jake Banks, Jay Armitage, Judy Wolff, Erin Sarofsky, Brad Tucker, Craig Duncan, Finnerty Steeves, Elizabeth Krajewski, Helena Bouchez, and all the other producers, cast, and crew members of Fortune Hunter, seaQuest 2032, and From the Earth to the Moon.

"Who is not delighted when finding strong words and sentiments from our youth—to help gauge before and after, to reinforce our paths, to reassure our personal direction? I am amazed at Roger's ability to consider these things and follow the play: To allow pluses and minuses to add flavor to the game! I am completely enamored with the thought of my brother at the beginning of this journey facing off with my brother who wrapped this project. I can picture their grins and joy quite clearly." —**Scott Darnell**, *Inventor*

"Roger Darnell has captured a way to share his personal childhood memories while sparking in each reader their own. His latest effort is a delightful use of poetry as a vehicle to tell a coming-of-age story." —**Katherine Bacon**, *Communication Goddess*

"Darnell guides us through a fascinating life of someone who had but one burning desire: to be a published writer. Undeniably, he proves that perseverance pays. Enjoy going on this journey from wannabe author to accomplished creator of the written word." —**Coach Ralph Barrett**, *Osceola Florida District Teacher of the Year*

"Roger takes us along on his life's journey as he pursues and succeeds at living his dream as a creative writer of poems, TV/movie screenplays, and PR marketing communications. As an industry mentor, Roger's book also provides a rich blueprint illuminating the way for aspiring freelance writers. While professional writing has brought him financial gains and fulfillment, the book conveys how writing is his passion and art, and something he's driven to do to connect with others and for the good of his soul." —**Claudia Kienzle**, *Writer*

"In Roger Darnell's Arc of the Poet, I really enjoyed the connection to his family and how being exposed to having a writer in his family moved him to write. I feel like people like myself who do not write consistently must miss out on a lot of good memories. Readers are sure to enjoy exposure to Roger's poetry, and hopefully the notion that writing as a practice helps keep us connected to our own lives . . . and in looking back, the history that exists within each of us." —**Katrina Cummings Stoll**, *Teacher*

"For anyone who's ever doubted themselves or questioned their purpose in life, Roger reminds us of just how far the discipline of tenacity can take you. His journey is one of constant discovery, vulnerability, and being shared through tender prose and stories of a life richly lived."—**Michele Kumar**, *CEO, Priya PR, Inc.*

"Every poem tells a story, and in this case Roger's timely poetry accompanies the narrative of his personal and professional journey. The poetry offers an emotional insight to events in his life while also showing his growth as a writer over time." —**Timothy Steinouer**, *Creative Producer*

"No matter how hard they try, the artist, the musician, and the author have no choice but to paint, to play, to write. The same is true of the poet, which explains why Roger Darnell had no choice but to pursue his passion. A career in the arts can be a lonely, frustrating, humbling, and exasperating experience, which makes the story of his journey so intriguing—and impressive."—**Gary McKechnie**, *Speaker, Author, Motojournalist*

"Our dreams rarely look the way we thought they would. Roger shows us a beautiful example of honoring, embracing, nurturing, and celebrating the dream that is."
—**Joan Zimmerman,** *MA, LMFT*

"In the years that I knew him best, I only have thought about how much I learned from Roger Darnell. His personal story is shared in this book, and his creative soul is laid bare. I will never look upon the memories of the creative time described in the book the same. Bravo Roger!" —**Bill Waxler,** *Production Designer*

"Writers, or aspiring writers of any variety, will draw encouragement, inspiration and insights from Roger Darnell's Arc of the Poet. Tracing his journey through the many diverse realms of creative writing, some of which paid the bills while others fed the soul, this book shines a light on what it means to be a poet, a working professional and a family man as well. Buy it; read it. You'll learn a bit about Roger and probably yourself as well. And you'll get to read some really fine poetry!"
—**Dick Wilson,** *Writer*

"As I read Arc of the Poet I found myself relating to multiple experiences. Before I knew it, I started to go down my own memory lane, and rushing to get to the next chapter to read the next poem. I look forward to reading it again!"
—**Chenoa Lombardy-Carver**

"For those who are staking out their own journeys in the creative-industrial complex, this book is for you. Roger shows how someone with the soul of an artist can successfully and confidently navigate that world, and at the same time displays his own considerable artistic talents. The book also shows another side of the "industry" – one that includes people who care very much about art and soul, who respect and highly appreciate the extraordinary courage of poets and artists everywhere."—**Dr. John Minbiole,** *Assistant Teaching Professor, Penn State University*

"Having known Roger Darnell from our U.S. Air Force Reserve time together, I had to reflect on how reading his Arc of the Poet was a testament to all three of the Air Force values of integrity, service and excellence that he and I as airmen adhered to during our time in service. I saw clearly in his memoir how his integrity never wavered regardless of the literary rejections he received. I was moved by Roger's firm adherence to his moral and artistic values that were so evident in his words. With that said, I salute him for this moving memoir."
—**Lt. Colonel Thomas Gammon,** *U.S. Air Force Reserve (Retired)*

ARC
OF THE
POET

A Poetic Memoir

ROGER DARNELL

TABLE OF CONTENTS

FOREWORD
Leslie "Jinx" Caulfield

One of the greatest rewards a teacher can achieve is watching a former student achieve his or her own great accomplishments. I taught drama, theatre and related subjects for over 30 years at the high school and college levels. For a lot of high school boys, the drama club and activities just weren't cool so it wasn't often I was able to coax a talented, good looking "leading man" type into the fold. One thing I remember about Roger was that he was confident enough in himself that he rarely, if ever, depended on others to gauge his "coolness"; he was too busy soaking up arts and literature. And while I spent my high school years trying to impress anyone, Roger's ambivalence and refusal to conform to teen herd mentality impressed everyone.

Roger's Arc of the Poet book is, to me, reminiscent of several first person accounts that chronicle the ups and downs, the trials and tribulations, the day to day struggle to carve out and maintain a wonderful joyous family life while never taking one's eye off of the promised dream/goal; a goal seemingly always just centimeters beyond our grasp. For many of us the struggle is real. Roger is undoubtedly the Little Engine That Could. It is often so much easier to quit swimming upstream past the sharp rocks and bears and instead slide back down into the relative calm of the familiar river below with its quiet eddies and peaceful pools.

Roger's prose flows easily throughout. His poetry is purposeful and imaginative. There is even a wonderful exercise for budding and advanced poets and writers. Roger calls it Ramble. Kerouac talks about life on the road and leaving friends behind for new adventures. He describes this experience as looking in the rearview mirror as he pulls away and everyone getting smaller and smaller until they disappear and it's time to look forward again. Ramble is a bit like that and Roger's writings remind me that life is temporary as are all things—and details become more beautiful and profound when viewed through the eyes of a poet.

June, 2022
Winter Park, Florida

1

Life Poetry

First published: February 22, 2011

TO BE PERFECTLY HONEST, I'm not sure that I'm capable of summarizing my childhood in just a few lines, but I do want to paint enough of a picture here to be able to show the ways poetry factored into my early life and came to be something I saw as my ticket to success. Here goes.

Like all kids of the late 1960s, I was exposed early and often to Dr. Seuss, and those fantastic rhymes of his really made deep impressions on me. However, there were other rhymes my older brother and I were exposed to, which had accompanied my mother's upbringing in a rural setting in Southern Illinois, at the hands of her Tennessee-born parents. From early ages, we heard this favorite time and again, inspiring our many adventures in the woods, and framing them in our minds.

Out in the forest there's a great big tree
with a hole in the middle that just fits me
so I climb inside and pretend I'm a bear
and I growl and I grumble and I rumble there.

Mom also performed a special version of Humpty Dumpty, where we'd sit on her knees until she'd get to the "fall," when she'd (gently) let us tumble to the ground, and finish the rhyme with a smiling flourish, and a big tickle.

For my older brother Scott and me, our early years involved a lot of moving. Although we nearly always returned to Greenville, Illinois, within a matter of months, we would head off to somewhere else, as our industrious dad pursued new career opportunities.

Whenever Dad was around, our family seemed to do pretty well together. We had many adventures, usually involving boats and bodies of water. Unfortunately, his career always seemed to keep him away from home, and eventually, Mom realized she just wasn't happy. Looking back, she often seemed to be writing during those evenings, using a typewriter she brought home. After her own father passed away, her marital commitment to our dad dissolved. Her administrative skills were soon sharp enough to put her back to work on her own. I was eight and Scott was 10 when we learned about divorce firsthand . . . and in the days that followed, living in St. Cloud, Florida, my mother refashioned herself.

It's very easy to color those days with our main activities: school, baseball, long summers, and Scott moving back and forth between our parents. However, when I think about my mom during those times, I think of her searching inwardly, and writing these poems that represented her actual means for coping with life. She had written scores of poems during the early days of child-rearing—"Scott Alan, Age Three" and "Roger—Three Years Old" were ones we cherished, loving our starring roles within our mother's clever verses. The poems of those years following the divorce were something else; those were not shared. Rather, they were her secret scrolls of hard-earned wisdom, apparently just meant for private study.

By the time I turned 13, I started having some original ideas about poetry, writing, personal values, and my self. Here's one of my first poems. I don't recall exactly when I wrote it, but I know it was before my 13th birthday, and after watching a Western film that set me off.

INVASION

"This is my land; it was so from the start,
and if you steal it from me, you'll steal my very heart."

"Well, now the land is mine—my wish is your command.
We'll give you a piece of desert; you can build up from the
   sand."

"But what of our wild buffalo, our sacred burial ground . . .
will you take from us all the good things we have found?"

"We have no need for buffalo, nor grounds of buried dead.
We'll clear land for new buildings. That's all that needs be
   said."

Looking back today, I'm seeing that poetry arose within me as a means for connecting meaningfully with my mother and demonstrating my writing abilities to her . . . and in the fact that I was using it to deal with life. I know she was the first person to see that poem, most others I have written since, and even this entry online. As I progressed on through high school and began shaping my own adult life, poetry helped me put things in perspective, and grow. The feedback I received meant a great deal to me, and eventually I came to feel that I could become famous, and accomplish all my lofty personal ambitions, through poetry.

2

Tour de Force

First published: March 3, 2011

BETWEEN 1978 AND 1989, I went from 12 to 23 . . .
from wondering about being a man to being one.

    I have a short stack of decent poetic writings from
those days, and as you'd expect, they are about things like love,
friends, and life's big events, positive and otherwise. I moved
each year of high school . . . from Greenville my freshman year
(Scott's sensational senior one) to Chattanooga, Tennessee,
then Ft. Lauderdale, Florida. When her second marriage
ended, Mom and I moved to Orlando for what was to be my
senior year, and her career phase next. With so much moving,
a lot of my writing was about what I believe T.S. Eliot called
"melancholy." As my studies continued, I gained some new
influences. A. E. Housman is still a favorite, discovered during
the Advanced Placement English class I lucked into that year,

where I learned so much about things I care about, courtesy of Mrs. Alice Wright and great writers like Ernest Hemingway, John Steinbeck, Aldous Huxley, George Orwell, Ralph Waldo Emerson, Thomas Hardy, and so many others.

I moved out right after I turned 18, and began making my own way in Orlando. I joined the U.S. Air Force Reserve and was in boot camp in San Antonio for my 19th birthday on May 5, 1985. That summer, I returned to Orlando and started college, and by the time I graduated in December, 1990, my six-year Air Force enlistment was done.

My experiences in the military were important in my writing, and another recurring subject over time has been my bro. As we grew up, we came to appreciate each other even more, while also regularly butting heads. I think we both had some rough edges when it came to interpersonal relationships, so it's good we've had each other for study material.

Here's a poem I wrote for Scott back in 1989.

BROTHER

Having tried, in times before,
to embellish our folklore
and to capture once in words
things our brotherhood incurs

we have somehow fallen short.
Yet, we gather our support
from the confidence we share
simply knowing other's there.

That's enough. It does us fine.
We both walk our separate line.
But, at least, we've had our fun,
and we'll have more 'fore we're done.

Take good care along your walks.
Though you're there, you're here in thoughts
giving strength through every wake.
We are one as breath we take.

I also wanted to share one other piece of my creative writing here, written in close proximity to that one. Along with many other writings I'm very proud of, the poem above ultimately wound up in a collection I pulled together in 1990 entitled "Just." The poem below is the second-to-last in that manuscript. Also written in 1989, six years later it provided my greatest opportunity to-date in the literary world, and my biggest challenge. At one time I had much higher hopes for this, but anyway, here is its unceremonious world premiere. I hope you enjoy it.

THE GONDOLIERS SING LOVE SONGS

Hand in hand, my fiancee and I walk the streets of Venice.
The gondoliers sing love songs, and we reminisce–
Rejoicing in growing together . . . despairing in growing apart.

Hand in hand, my lover and I stroll the streets of Venice.
The gondoliers sing love songs, and we search the silence–
As two silent rivers run beneath the surficial choir.

Hand in hand, my first love and I survey the streets of Venice.
The gondoliers sing love songs, and we are children again—
Unable to move in fear of breaking the virginal, sacred vows.

Hand in hand, my prospect and I serenade the streets of
    Venice.
The gondoliers sing love songs, and we are their chivalrous
    companions.
Awkward in our hand clasp, we spy upon the other couples.

Pen in hand, my imagination and I wander the streets of
    Venice.
The gondoliers sing love songs, but I cannot hear them.
Wherein does love become an everlasting aspect of life?

Hand in hand, I stand alone on the edge of the world.
The gondoliers of Venice are far away; so, too, are their love
    songs.
And I know I can write love—and sing it—but can I keep it?

3

True Love

First published: March 10, 2011

EVEN BEFORE 1990 HAD OFFICIALLY BEGUN, I recall feeling anxious for it to be over. It truly was an endurance test for me, involving one marathon ordeal after another. I turned 23 that year, with no fanfare, and I took that as a sign of maturity. I also persevered in seizing my military and college experiences with the best of my thoughts and abilities, which I saw as evidence of my growing strength and confidence. By the time it ended, 1990 gave me a great deal in return for all my efforts.

Looking back now, 21 years later, I think my determination to forge my own career path as a freelance professional is the richest of many valuable life lessons I carried into 1990. For that reason, I now have extra appreciation for this poem I stopped to write back on December 30,

1989. Its final stanza puts that important mindset into clear perspective.

IN THE DISTANCE

Through your vast and piled aspects,
on a blurred or focused day,
think of these few polished crystals
thence, politely, clear the way:

There's a place for you in Oxford;
you'll be welcomed at the gates;
you'll have children ever-thankful
for your handling of their fates;

many pages pouring reverence
will abound upon your shelf;
you'll have movies made about you
next to ones you've made yourself;

words of honor you have written,
such as Drake McCawber's tale,
will run 'cross the lips of mothers,
blazing children lovely trail;

but the most important keepsake
you should cherish on a day
owes to strength and faith from living
only in your chosen way.

Another idea I embraced during those days was that there's no such thing as defeat, only education. In January, I set my sights on graduating in December with two B.A. degrees. In the course of earning the 33 upper-level college credits necessary to pull that off, I took on new duties with my Air Force Reserve unit, and worked as a freelance word processor and audiovisual stage-hand. All that work barely kept me above the poverty level, but my motivations were clear; since every choice was completely self-driven, I was determined to succeed.

Through all these experiences, I was being graded by instructors, supervisors in many industries, military officers, professionals stretching from the top to the bottom of the creative industry, and even editors and readers at my university's newspaper. For the last 16 months before graduating, I wrote a weekly humor column entitled "Observations." Looking over the journal I kept, I can see that one day in October, the editor in chief told me point blank: "I think some of what you write is shit." I cut myself some slack, knowing how hard I had to work to write those columns, but took her criticism on the chin, and kept on learning and trying to improve.

Fortunately, a few key positive developments shaped up, too, and together with the unwavering support from my family, my good friend and roommate Jay Lerew, and many other close friends, that proved to be all I needed. My humor column helped me win a Scripps Howard Foundation Fellowship . . . but much more importantly, it also helped me win the heart of an amazing girl named Beth Ann Kiefert.

Friends, I am very proud to say that the addition of this young lady into my life is the key ingredient in the joyous, rewarding life walk I've been enjoying ever since.

From June through August that year, Beth took off with a few friends to backpack across Europe. Ultimately, that period was intensely productive for me, as I maniacally threw myself into one duty or commitment after another, trying my best to stay busy until her return. I set goals to write a novella, a full-length screenplay, and a collection of my poetry specifically for children. Although none of those projects came together during those weeks, I did organize my poems chronologically, type them up and begin preparing a few submissions for local writing competitions.

By the time December was ending, I had collected my diplomas and my Honorable Air Force discharge, and started building a new life with the girl of my dreams. Suddenly, my next-level goals were coming within reach. At that magical moment in time, I saw literary recognition and success as one possible path to financial freedom, which I felt would allow me to read and write to my heart's content. While I also had to recommit to the opportunities I could line-up as a freelance wage-earner, I began mounting serious efforts to get my creative writing into print. Guiding and supporting my ambitions was this beautiful, energetic, vivacious girl, who that year gave me the most prized of worldly possessions for keeps: true love.

OUR LOVE-LONG COZY FIRES

I looked all through a book of verse
but nowhere in its authors' terse
elaborations did it grace
a rhyme I felt could fill this space.

Where once no words had seen the sun
I've thought to build a sprightly, fun,
and pointed piece with loving point:
To wound your heart—but then anoint

it—with a potion made from scratch,
the contents: all of me. A patch,
hand-sewn by all the powers that be
will heal your heart, and render "we."

I hope a poem can make such mark—
can leap from page to fire such spark!—
for, should these markings do their work
your love for me will go berserk!

And nowhere, save within my grasp
e'er will your fancy think to pass.
My Beth, you're all my heart desires . . .
here's to our love-long cozy fires.

4

Spinning Out

First published: March 17, 2011

From the great poem *East Coker* written by "American-born English" poet T.S. Eliot.

Home is where one starts from. As we grow older
The world becomes stranger, the pattern more complicated
Of dead and living. Not the intense moment
Isolated, with no before and after,
But a lifetime burning in every moment
And not the lifetime of one man only
But of old stones that cannot be deciphered.

THE FREEDOM I ENJOYED immediately after earning two bachelor's degrees and completing my six-year Air Force Reserve commitment was wonderfully liberating, and my girlfriend Beth and I pressed ahead into our whirlwind adventures. My tiny backyard garage apartment in downtown Orlando became her home, too, over time, as we grew together. Meanwhile, facing our college debts, we both dedicated ourselves to earning paychecks.

Beth also earned her communications degree at the end of 1990, and by that time, she was already a seasoned bartender at the highly popular Bennigan's Grill and Tavern in Casselberry. Right after graduating, she landed an apartment industry job in sales and management. That opportunity and others to follow were solid and stable, if sometimes stressful . . . but she jumped right in and thrived.

For me, the career path was much more erratic and hard to trace. In essence, I persevered in trying to open doors and earn the credits necessary to do the type of work I wanted to do (any skilled, challenging work in the film and television industry, with a preference for research, writing, and production), while clocking all the $10 hours I could book as an experienced clerical or audiovisual freelancer.

During a final college course, one professor told us all that as soon as we graduated, we'd be ready for entry-level jobs. At the time, the thought that everything I was going through to graduate was just a prerequisite for something "entry level" felt like being punched in the face. I felt strongly, and probably expressed my thoughts out loud: "What are you talking about? I do not need a college degree to get an entry-level job!"

Maybe I was technically right about that, but my first months after graduation proved that the types of more senior jobs I felt qualified for were beyond my reach. While trying to hold out for some interesting work on a film production or somehow shape-up a worthwhile solitary or joint-effort project through my resourcefulness, I did send out quite a few resumes and cover letters to apply for full-time jobs. I recall that one was for a communications position for Florida's State Parks . . . which would have been fun if an offer had come through. None did.

As a backup, I put another plan into action. Coming into 1991, I had prepared a few polished submissions from my original poetry for writing contests. My hope—and also my expectation—was that the "Just" manuscript would win a major contest. When the correspondence arrived with icy reports featuring others' names as winners, I was crushed, humiliated, and left to seriously consider: *How did I not win?*

All things considered, those days were challenging in a lot of ways. Usually I was racing back and forth across Orlando's byways in pursuit of work, then landing at odd times at home on Meridale Avenue, where Beth and I would reconnect, get recharged, and then head off again in separate directions. In the quiet moments, I would ponder my next literary moves, and try to assess all the ways my artistic efforts, diligence, preparation, practice, and polish fell short. Of course, looking through that microscope, I was really examining every facet of my life and trying to figure out what to do next to lead myself in the right direction.

Although I felt my career was "going nowhere fast" at that time, Beth and I held our own, and in the process, we enjoyed so many simple things together that not achieving instant literary fame became more acceptable. To my great fortune, she was always perfectly okay with me for who I was, and of course, it also helped a ton that her dad was constantly reminding me that "life is good" (even before it was on t-shirts), and cautioning me, "Don't forget to stop to smell the flowers!" Like my own mother, he was always very encouraging to me, and Beth's mom, step-dad, brothers, sisters, and all her friends also joined the growing support group that gave me a lot of self-respect to build on. Their positive examples and feedback trained me to begin appreciating everything life has to offer, while I kept my sites set on the entertainment industry, and continued to aim high.

Over the next few years, I became something of a fixture at Orlando's downtown library, while studying and collecting the works of great classical and contemporary writers and artists in my spare time, and writing. Through research, I learned I needed to get better if I wanted my poetry to appear in The New Yorker, The Paris Review, and other high-profile targets I identified.

While originally my literary aspirations were driven by dreams of fame and fortune, my mom made a very important point with the following not-so-subtle newspaper clipping. As the editors at the New York Times Book Review "Noted With Pleasure," writing poetry is not really a viable money-making proposition. It was a great lesson for sure, but as you'll see, it took awhile for it to sink into my head.

From Sam Hamill's essay "Shadow Work," from his 1990 Broken Moon Press book, "A Poet's Work: The Other Side of Poetry": *Poetry is not commerce. It is not something to be exchanged or traded. It is a gift to the poet, a gift for which the poet, eternally grateful, spends a lifetime in preparation, and which the poet, in turn, gives away and gives away again. The actual work of preparation is shadow work: it must be performed without thought of money, and it is 'essential' work in that it enables the poet to recognize and accept the gift and, in giving the gift away, do so with a great accompanying energy. But that energy, that experience we name poem, cannot be traded in the marketplace because it cannot be subverted. It won't light a lightbulb, run a heater or an air conditioner or a microwave oven. It is only a poem—necessary, and inviolable, an articulation of a world beyond the possibilities of money.*

5

Wake-Up Call

First published: March 24, 2011

WE KEPT THE AFTERBURNERS ON and blasted into 1991, with me clawing my way forward professionally and growing up further alongside my sweetheart. I wrote an original short script for producer/ director Bill Waxler, and his plans to produce it brought together a very talented group of production professionals and friends. Entitled "Bumper Crop," that project gained steam through the spring, and by late June, we were on-location, ready to shoot it on 16mm film.

"Bumper Crop" is about an older man who awakens from a dream that shines a new light on a long-held misconception which had affected him deeply throughout his life. Finally understanding that he was not responsible for his brother's accident long ago, his awakening represents a new lease on life.

Early on June 29, a wonderful group of people gathered at a vacant roadside gas station in Sanford, Florida, to begin shooting. Little did I know that, later that day, while we were trying to get our shots, my own brother would suffer his own life-changing accident, after diving into Greenville's Governor Bond Lake.

It was about 1:30 AM on Sunday when my mother called with the news that led from one thing to the next. In those hours, I didn't know if I would ever have the chance to talk to my one and only brother again. By Monday, I was at the hospital and hearing the dark forecast—never walk again, life hanging on by a thread. Thankfully, my big brother survived all that, and though he doesn't walk, he stands above most people I know as an amazingly resourceful, industrious, upbeat person who is a pillar of my family and the town of Greenville, among many other sterling achievements. Still, on July 1, 1991, I had a rough night trying to sleep in a hospital waiting room. I had Spalding Gray's "Swimming to Cambodia" to read, and for my therapy, I wrote this poem.

JOHN WAYNE DIES AGAIN

A larger-than-life figure steps from the lights
into heaven's shadowy smoking area.
FLICK! the metal clicks open to bare
the wick—flint scrapes—FIRE
illuminates the deep lines of the Duke.
The fire alights upon the fine tobacco—dances
an orange-red tap-dance in his eyes.
CLICK! The lighter disappears.
He looks on.

A couple has joined friends high atop
a boathouse. He is a champion among men—
she his equal opposite. A live-wire dances
dangerously between them: a glint in her
eye which he catches, which says she
doesn't believe him.

The Duke pulls long and hard . . .
smoke swirls around his head.

It's a game the two play. He maintains
control by streaming constant effluent her
way . . . teasing. She teases back. He pretends
to be entertained, but quietly seethes. She doesn't
know him as well as she thinks!—can't have
his control!

The Duke pulls long and hard . . .
red veins surge in his squinting eyes.

She breaks eye contact, turns to the friend.
She acts like she's not even thinking about me,
he tells himself. She knows she's always
been wrong before. He JUMPS a bit in his
chair. Her eyes SPIN to find him—just
teasing her again. She knits her eyebrows,
turns back to the meaningless conversation.

The Duke pulls long and hard—
smoking cherry burning hardened fingers.

BOOM! he launches. Feet measure, place,
push, to the railing, momentum top-heavy
and no-doubt sailing from the height toward
lake's small chops. My God! She'll laugh—
she'll know I'm her DANGEROUS man—
I WIN! But look at that water, man!
Dive shallow—pull up!

The Duke pinches the butt off, smashes
the burning part into the charred floor.

Meanwhile, the orange-red flickering
in the eyes dies out. Nevermore,
perhaps, will the crushed bone, the
wasted nerve-center burn his fingers.
John Wayne dies again.

That writing was an attempt to pacify my thoughts in the midst of so much sadness, fear, and frustration. Scott's girlfriend Rachel, my parents and many other close family members were there, also suffering through those first nights, trying to comfort Scott and each other, as various doctors, specialists, and nurses delivered updates that were anything but reassuring. But in the main bout, Scott's body and mind were fighting for life, and we all tried to help in whatever small ways we could, hoping for a miracle.

One wise leap I made soon thereafter was proposing to Beth. She said yes, and my life's been getting better ever since. The positive effect kicked-in right away: Immediately upon returning from our engagement trip to the Bahamas, I was hired by a feature film development company to help package, sell, and produce a remake of "Flipper."

In the meantime, Scott moved through all the steps of stabilization and rehab in various St. Louis-area hospitals, with constant help and support from Rachel, back-up from my dad and step-mom, and semi-regular visits by my mom, who lived in Florida, like us. Everything was hard on Scott, but through his unbelievable strength, perseverance, and determination, he rocked onward, encouraging each of us to carry on with our own lives . . . and freeing us to do so.

For a long time after "John Wayne Dies Again," I did not write much poetry . . . but I did read a lot. Just around that time, my friend Hardy Edwards introduced me to the writing of Charles Bukowski. I began reading all the Buk books I could get my hands on, and his constant references to other fine writers led my literary and musical interests in exciting and fun new directions.

Bless you for making it this far in my bard's tale: Please accept my deepest thanks. You are among a few people of whom I am very proud. Of all the wonderful, powerful artists I encountered by age 24, Buk made me realize how very much I had to learn, all while putting a smile on my face, which remains even now. I soon came to love this most unusual man, and even received a letter from him one day.

6

Serious Dreams

First published: April 2, 2011

COMING INTO 1992, I was living a dream: working in development for Ivan Tors Entertainment at Disney-MGM Studios, and hopeful that the screenplay I was writing for their lead feature film project would launch my career as a screenwriter. But on May 5, the day I turned 26, I was laid off and asked to clean out my office in Bungalow 3 and turn in my backlot pass. Though it was a serious setback, I landed in decent shape, mainly because Beth was in my life. Later that month, together with legions of family members and friends, we experienced a glorious wedding amid the cornfields and Spring-time Illinois countryside, surrounded by love.

That era is one I look back on with a lot of pride . . . and disappointment; I really had high hopes of landing a major role in the movie business, and by that February, the path to success appeared right before my eyes. I thought I was well on my way.

Through my boss at Tors, I quickly came into contact with leaders at every major talent agency, countless successful independent and studio filmmakers, the best actors and craftspeople, and even Roy Disney, Dick Cook, and Jeffrey Katzenberg. Along with writing a first pass on the "Flipper: The Movie" screenplay (where the story was not of my choosing at all) that was photocopied and sent off everywhere so fast it made my head spin, I also wrote and produced a marketing presentation that was screened and applauded by the aforementioned Disney royalty.

Meanwhile, over the course of eight months on the studio backlot, my colleagues and I were constantly on display to the endless tourists who beheld us from trams, and through giant panel windows looking into soundstages, production offices, and post-production facilities. In the snapshots and home movies of too many tourists to count, we were the stars living the dream life, there among the Mickey Mouse topiaries, props, and set pieces. That kingdom was proclaimed to be Hollywood East, and being inside was empowering.

That February, I was invited out to UCF to talk to a group of film students, and I gave them an earful, mixing encouragement with the type of canned pessimism you just can't escape in "the industry." Among many wise words, I shared some from the book "Making Money in Film and Video: A Freelancer's Handbook, by industry luminary Raul Da Silva.[1]

1 Da Silva, Raul, "Making Money in Film and Video: A Freelancer's Handbook," Focal Press, 1992.

In the passage I read, Mr. Da Silva makes the case for the production business being very hard to enter. Citing thousands of academic institutions teaching related subjects, he then explained that most opportunities fall under communications, not entertainment. Finally, he concluded that scriptwriting and a solid understanding of both business and marketing were the true keys to success in the most accessible realms of the industry.

I also have a letter I wrote to my brother at that time, where I spilled out my excitement over the fact that renowned director, producer, cinematographer, and screenwriter Peter Hyams was at that time reviewing my draft of the Flipper screenplay, along with my detailed research notes. Sadly, over the following weeks, deals failed to materialize . . . and as new investors gained control of the project's rights, my clear path vanished. Four years later, "Flipper" got made, starring Paul Hogan and Elijah Wood, and credited to many others.

Cut loose in May, 1992, Beth and I sailed into planning our wedding, and almost 19 years later, it is still a vivid and cherished memory for us and our loved ones. After our week-long honeymoon in a cabin in North Georgia, we came back home, picked up the pieces, and set out again. While scoring paychecks through staff and freelance jobs in the industry over the next year, I remained very serious about my literary aspirations. Some of the marketing experience I gained at Ivan Tors and through freelance writing gigs gave me a new angle. I wrote a story that appeared in Videography magazine, and soon began pursuing assignments with other industry trade publications. Encouraged by my success with nonfiction writing submissions, I renewed efforts to submit various poetry collections into contests, while also writing short and feature-length dramatic screenplays, and even more commercials, PSAs, and scripts for marketing videos. Also, I continued to correspond with different literary agents, trying to gain representation, and getting some positive feedback along the way.

In the previous entry for this series, I mentioned receiving a letter from Charles Bukowski. My friend Hardy Edwards had asked me to write a screenplay based on certain Bukowski poems, and then, to try to get it cleared for promotional use. My early diplomatic efforts generated the briefest of missives: "Let this serve as notice that you are not within your rights," signed by Bukowski himself. We did eventually get his permission to submit Hardy's finished short film into a local festival, but earning the scorn of an artist I so admired was yet another humbling experience from 1992.

Through it all and into 1993, my life at home with Beth continued to be wonderfully rewarding. With her by my side, I kept dreaming big. While I wasn't yet able to give her the security she deserved, I worked hard, and expressed my devotion using all the energy and artistry I could muster. In May of 1993, that involved some writing combined with my amateur filmmaking skills, using original photographs, a Super 8 movie shot back in 1990, a borrowed 8mm camcorder, and an audio cassette deck. The resulting video was quite personal, but we're all friends here. Here are the words.

BLACK AND WHITE

Words can't make the stillness
the windswept rooftop
where
our love doth lie
our nap on that day gave me so much
it took my words away
there's nothing to say play pray
it's all inside
everyone knows
without me telling

i love you.

7

Home Stretch

First published: April 2, 2011

NEARLY A YEAR after our spectacular wedding, May of 1993 found me, Beth, and pretty much everyone else in our family continuously thinking about my brother, his daily perseverance in recovering from his July '91 diving accident, and his successful return to a more normal lifestyle. By then, he and his girlfriend had their own place, on my dad and step-mom's farm and within earshot of their home. From every angle, Scott was making us all very proud, and showing the kind of resounding inner strength we all hope to have when faced with unimaginable adversity.

At one point right after the accident, my mom wondered aloud if we would ever be happy again. Illinois has always provided a powerful attraction for me around my birthday in May, and I was especially thankful while driving there on May

6, 1993, that I was feeling real joy. Here's a poem I wrote back in 1988 about those annual treks to my native homeland.

THE DIFFERENT DRUMMER

I don't know why I had to go
Back home in summer's early glow . . .
But in my feeble state of mind
I felt a loss I had to find.

The great escape some said I made—
And true: to sense the solemn shade
Of home, and leave the world behind
Which made me cold and scared and blind.

In all pursuits I pushed myself
Beyond the pack that somehow shelve
Their hopes and dreams for social norm
And fear the lonesome, ruthless storm.

In battle-youth, I made my way
Through acid rain of dream decay,
And while the storm's calm eye drew near
My bravery was turned to fear.

With summoned strength I fled the storm
And limped in semi-shattered form
Toward the place where life began
To find The Answer to The Man.

I found the place I've always known:
Aunts, uncles, grandmas, cousins grown,
The trees that fell that I know well,
Whose echoes clang a rusty bell.

The native country took me in—
It mattered not where I had been;
It saw me as I was, and still
Gave praise for all my vital will.

I rested there and took my time.
I slept amid the dew-cool thyme.
Serene, I saw what life could be . . .
Then spread my wings and flew off, free.

I don't know just what made me go
Back home in summer's early glow . . .
But on the heartfelt, wholesome track
I found my strength and brought it back.

The reputation of my mom's mom—known as Granny Bea or Aunt Bea to most, Mrs. Ridings to everyone else—reached far and wide from the beautiful spot she and my grandfather had settled in long before. Called Terrapin Ridge and located near Greenville, the rural area feels a lot more like their own ancestral Tennessee homeland than Illinois. Until she passed away in 2001, those woods surrounding their home were enchanted by Granny Bea's warmth, charm and grace. Even now, when we return to the area, we are pulled that direction . . . but it was different when she was there awaiting us in her legendary kitchen: friends and family-members all made bee-lines there every chance we got, and nothing could deter us from those visits.

Scott and I were also very tight with my dad's mom, whom he had dubbed "Bam" at an early age. She also was always very happy to see and feed us, and we both loved her dearly. She had remarried and moved to nearby Keyesport, and helping get Scott there and to Granny Bea's place were at the top of my May '93 trip's agenda. It took a lot of hands, and the usual oversized dose of determination from Scott, but those experiences came together colorfully, and they meant a lot to each of us, and to many others who weren't there but who heard about our visits through various grapevines.

After making that journey where I spent so much time with my bro, and then returning home, I was ready to face my most ambitious objectives with renewed energy. I reviewed and polished all my creative writing, and after systematically assessing my media targets and their preferences in cross-reference with my stockpile, I printed lots of papers out and sent them flying to the four corners of the world, and all points in between. My inner artist also attempted to creatively channel my brother in the following experimental essay. It appears here for the first time, even though I began sending it to literary media outlets almost as soon as it was finished.

WORDSWORTH

I can only sit in this chair beside this window right now and contemplate the form my body's taken.

How do I love thee? As the foggy numb day meanders through the moist panes; as the bird-shape stirs effortlessly outside. I've been paralyzed for two years now. I love thee as the guy inside a window, hidden from your awareness.

My paralysis is really the last thing I ever try to think about, which explains why I'm dwelling on it now.

One second of television is all it takes. In that fast flash I am put in my place—pitted in my sensational existence. It's a shell often heavier than I can carry. It's a bear trap clamped onto my ass—even my soul! For two years I've thought about how to get out of it. Today I realize that maybe I never will—or, at least, that I'm currently powerless against it, and this field of vision has not so far illuminated many suitable prospects.

If you're an adventurer, imagine with me any one second of television. Focus in on one taut muscle, or one well-trimmed mustache. Journey one slow, moveable olfactory feast along exquisite, lightly sweet neck-silk . . . one horse-drawn ride across the spraying surf.

Please let me clarify something: I'm not bittcr, I'm just writing. I don't want to make you suffer, I simply must grab what light I can find around the world—your light, for example—with my summoned strength. If even as vaguely as a distant wind caressing your cheek, inside I need to feel I have something to share. And, for me to have any chance of really touching you, you have to understand.

I'm just putting this here in case you're interested, because I've been a hell of a guy, all in all, and I'm still here! I can still sweep you off your feet. After all, you are talking to a star athlete and the pride of a good family. I deserve your attention.

God, I'm still here. Joseph Conrad wrote that we live as we dream: alone. Outside my room, in the halls, on the streets, in each of my parents' homes, in a few bars, in a couple of offices, there are people that help, and I wouldn't want them to take this wrong, but I am alone. You are alone. Occasionally we're together; always we're alone. These words offer hope, just as my brain still races despite the frozen sea south of the neckline.

I used to dive, as in off of a diving-board. Not professionally or anything. You should've seen me! From this watery reflection arise my most profound memories. Swimming around with my cousins with our masks and snorkels, picking up pennies from the bottom of a pool. In those blue underwater mental filings, I age in mask and snorkel. Beaten up in many surfs off many beaches, I once and finally addressed fear and stroked out bravely beyond the waves. I found something unbelievable out there. I can see it now: blue, purple, red, green. On coral formations you can discover it for yourself. You're part of the food chain. It's very humbling and it's real.

I had given up on ever finding a buried treasure, but on a reef, I clearly realized my place, weighed my capabilities, and bet everything on my ability to survive. It worked. Some treasure, huh? It's yours.

Outer space? It's an ocean that includes each of us. I've learned all about it. Outer space offers me a TV sticking out of a wall, up where I can see it from my bed, my planter, my wheat field. This, for the time being, is me. This and the people that walk through that door, shining or scuffing the slick linoleum, as the case may be.

This shall not last. I will walk again. Denial? Really, between friends, what do you know about it? Do you realize that you're part of the food chain, friend? Well, I do. Tears run down my window, as the day heats up outside. I'll be here, ignoring the endless fingers in my face.

Please, in all your activities, be careful. It doesn't really take much to find yourself inside this glass. The world has millions of false trails. Listen inside yourself for your pulse—it's certainly there—sounding an unmistakable alarm which tells you, no matter where you are, your life's only beginning.

Keep reading. Breeze toward something new now. Meanwhile, rest assured that the words I've poured you here can be better trusted than most you'll find. Your life is in your hands; proceed with caution.

My life, I cannot love you better.

8

Feedback

First published: April 16, 2011

EVEN BEFORE I had done any real research or taken my first steps into the legitimate literary world, the intellect, attitudes, and ideas I gained through my parents and early life experiences left me with an expansive sense of entitlement. One delusion I suffered from was believing that the first time my work was read by any sound judge of a literary competition, my name would be affixed to the prize and I'd be on my way to fame. By the midway point of 1993, however, my steady outreach to editors covering poetry and short fiction had only resulted in a growing collection of rejection slips. Most of them were just generic slips of paper, photocopied and stuck into the required SASE (self-addressed stamped envelope) without a second's thought . . . but others were from manuscript competitions where I had little choice but to accept that my work had actually been read and deemed unworthy.

As previously mentioned, I was thankful for having ventured into the area of nonfiction trade journals covering the film and television industry, and to have started hitting those marks. It was extremely satisfying seeing my byline in magazines that often had considerably larger circulations than any of the literary publications I was sending work to . . . and getting paid for those articles worked wonders for my professional reputation, confidence, and self-esteem.

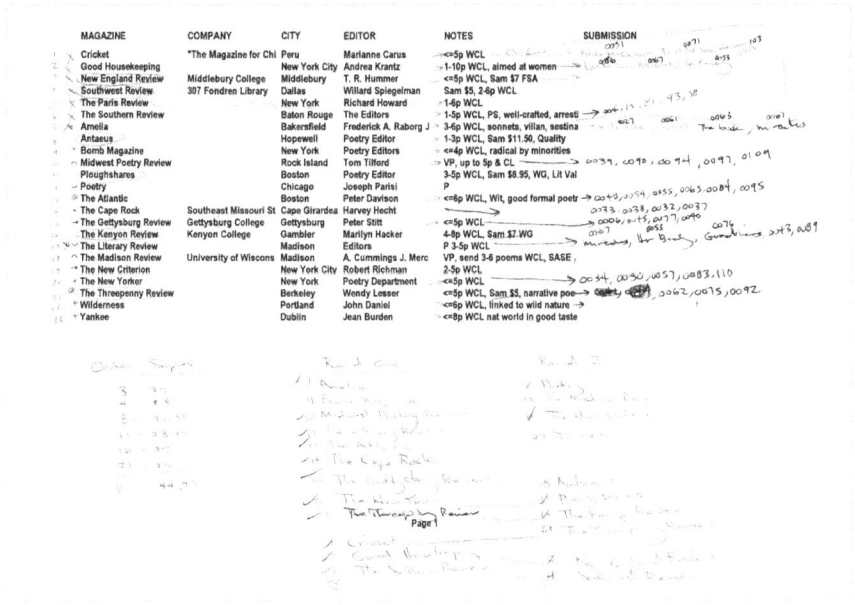

MAGAZINE	COMPANY	CITY	EDITOR	NOTES	SUBMISSION
Cricket	*The Magazine for Chi	Peru	Marianne Carus	<=5p WCL	
Good Housekeeping		New York City	Andrea Krantz	1-10p WCL, aimed at women	
New England Review	Middlebury College	Middlebury	T. R. Hummer	<=5p WCL, Sam $7 FSA	
Southwest Review	307 Fondren Library	Dallas	Willard Spiegelman	Sam $5, 2-6p WCL	
The Paris Review		New York	Richard Howard	1-6p WCL	
The Southern Review		Baton Rouge	The Editors	1-5p WCL, PS, well-crafted, arrest	
Amelia		Bakersfield	Frederick A. Raborg J	3-6p WCL, sonnets, villan, sestina	
Antaeus		Hopewell	Poetry Editor	1-3p WCL, Sam $11.50, Quality	
Bomb Magazine		New York	Poetry Editors	<=4p WCL, radical by minorities	
Midwest Poetry Review		Rock Island	Tom Tilford	VP, up to 5p & CL	
Ploughshares		Boston	Poetry Editor	3-5p WCL, Sam $8.95, WG, Lit Val	
Poetry		Chicago	Joseph Parisi	P	
The Atlantic		Boston	Peter Davison	<=8p WCL, Wit, good formal poetr	
The Cape Rock	Southeast Missouri St	Cape Girardea	Harvey Hecht	<=5p WCL	
The Gettysburg Review	Gettysburg College	Gettysburg	Peter Stitt	<=5p WCL	
The Kenyon Review	Kenyon College	Gambler	Marilyn Hacker	4-8p WCL, Sam $7 WG	
The Literary Review		Madison	Editors	P 3-5p WCL	
The Madison Review	University of Wiscons	Madison	A. Cummings J. Merc	VP, send 3-6 poems WCL, SASE	
The New Yorker		New York City	Robert Richman	2-5p WCL	
The New Criterion		New York	Poetry Department	<=5p WCL	
The Threepenny Review		Berkeley	Wendy Lesser	<=5p WCL, Sam $5, narrative poe	
Wilderness		Portland	John Daniel	<=6p WCL, linked to wild nature	
Yankee		Dublin	Jean Burden	<=8p WCL nat world in good taste	

Several of the trade stories I authored also featured my original photographs. They weren't anything great, but through those experiences I learned the importance of having good images to accompany any project I wanted to see into print. My education at UCF and in the Air Force gave me some serious instruction in photography, and on my own, I kept trying to improve those skills, along with my writing. I was especially proud of a series of snaps captured in Chicago back in 1990, and as I diligently continued researching literary journals and reaching out with new poetry and creative writings, I also made some attempts at placing my photos within those types of publications.

In June of '93, I was again invited back to UCF, this time at the invitation of beloved gentleman faculty member Keith Fowles, who asked me to speak to senior students in his Radio/TV and Society class. Having gained a more solid foothold in my career aspirations since my visit earlier that year, optimism took center stage: I assured everyone that there was certainly room for them in the industry, while encouraging them to set their goals, but then to be sure to revisit them often, considering the likelihood of change over time. Keith was very complimentary and appreciative, saying he felt it was a message his students needed to hear. That was a proud day.

Soon thereafter, with big help from my dad and step-mom, Beth and I bought our first home. Located in the charming downtown area of Orlando near Kaley Street, it was over 40 years old and offered less than 800 square feet of living space, but to us and our cat Maggie, it was a castle. Also, it featured a nice big lot, and four of the world's most beautiful and immense Live Oak trees.

With momentum favoring us, and my career affording some gratifying accolades, it's hard to describe exactly how I felt when I received several pages of photocopied "correspondence" in response to a poetry submission. When it came to magazine editors and established literary figures, I had received no feedback on my creative writing, and other than having my work accepted and put into print, that's what I wanted most. The two pages of glib poets' instructions I received from a highly acclaimed, Detroit-based poet and publisher hit me like a spiritual beat-down I could not ignore. The letter I wrote and mailed off in my response came from my heart, and it reflects some regrettable immaturity. What I admire about it is the rising self-assurance and composure I was beginning to find in aiming for the high road.

July 14, 1993

Thank you for the pages of poets' instructions you sent me, along with the poems I had sent you. I don't know what type of feedback you normally get from this process, but I thought I'd contribute mine.

The nice thing about your two pages is that it gives concrete means by which to address the world of poetry writing. However, as you are aware, a poet following all of your advice and addressing your observations might still produce refuse.

But I'm getting ahead of myself, and entering into a land where I have nothing to gain. I will simply say that your information included so much rhetoric as to certainly offend any writer who does, for a fact, own and read many books of poetry, attend readings, read magazines, read poetry-specific instruction books, labor through workshops, etc.

My suggestion: rather than saying, "I would like to point out some realities of which you may not be aware," it is my opinion (since this is a subjective world, is it not, with differing standards, styles, insights, and goals for as many editors in the world?) that your observations and advise might offend less were you to take the position, "I would like to share some of my insights after my ____ years in the realm of poetry."

For, as I read through your list of 20 items, my education in poetry illuminates the fact that for each, and especially for those you checked-off for me, there is an endless supply of published poems which defy your scope.

Thank you again for sharing this corner of your world of ideas on poetry. I have been doing my homework in poetry for 11 years, and I am an excellent student. I have prepared myself to become a publishable poet among the best of them. I'm sorry that my poems didn't make your socks go up and down. Perhaps I'll be in touch again some day.

Sincerely—Roger Darnell

9
Dear Departures
First published: May 28, 2011

N THE SUMMER OF 1993, I was very proud to be the husband of Beth Darnell, a home-owner in downtown Orlando, and a genuine communications industry professional making some headway as a writer, pro-ducer, and photojournal-ist. My campaign efforts pitching original creative entries into literary pub-lications produced no other significant results, until one day a poem came back with this note attached. I could have wept. Here's the poem it was attached to.

IF VIRTUE HAD TEETH

One day I stopped dusting my old trophies.
I stopped gluing them back together when they broke
And became kind of embarrassed for people to see them.
They used to mean so much to me.

One day, I'll get a big check as payment
For something I've written. Soon thereafter,
I'll look for another check, of higher value,
That may or may not ever come.

One day, fortune will smile on me.
I won't have to chase the elusive ghost of finance
And I'll breathe the fine air of freedom—
I react well to environmental changes.

One day, I will lay my pen down
For the last time. It may roll off to the ground
And I won't pick it up. I'll realize
What I've not written—and it won't matter.

Many days, I will continue to live without you
Facing the gray numbness, the envelope.
While I know that life is life, and I must cherish it,
My happiness, security, motivation, miss you.

One day I'll understand my primal longings.
I'll live the glorious days, and rarely recall
These soul searches. Although, I could be mistaken—
They might, eventually, mean a lot to me.

These words had been written several years earlier, during the summer of 1990, my last year at UCF. As documented in this arc, that was an excellent time for me; I had stayed busy, applied myself, and focused on the girl of my dreams—and some other very positive developments in my life. It's not one of the greatest poems I've ever written, but I feel it colorfully reflects some of the key virtues of my life at that time. I'm especially proud that it helped me make a connection with Tom Tilford, then-editor of Midwest Poetry Review, who with his kind note, gave my life new meaning.

The final poems I added into my first poetry manuscript also were written in 1990, so "If Virtue Had Teeth" was among a few I thought worth sharing in my newer era. Along with some other poems and shorts I wrote before receiving Tom's note above, it was included in two different collections I submitted into various competitions over the years to follow. Looking back on it now, after encountering so much indifference to my work, I see that Tom's note gave me the sense that someone was reading it . . . which suddenly made me look at everything I'd been submitting much more realistically. Later that summer, as I considered all the legitimately great literary writing widely evident through magazines, books, newspapers, and on cable TV and the radio, compared with what I had to offer, I was humbled.

Then, something unbelievable happened: a dear friend from my senior year of high school died. Dante Castellano was the great guy who befriended me in 1983 and helped me see the world from new heights. His family embraced me, too, and they were warm, wonderful, and tightly knit, as well as being very well-to-do. I was hurt when one day, my friendship was just dropped, but I carried on, forged ahead, and relied more on other friends. During the years that followed, I feel that if we'd seen each other again, we would have quickly built solid new bridges together, but we never had that opportunity. We had well over 1,000 in our 1984 graduating class from Oak Ridge High School . . . and in 1993, I learned how dear Dante had been to each of us. Especially knowing how much he had going for him, no one ever imagined his life would end so soon.

Along with many other Oak Ridge Pioneers and residents of Orlando, I marched forward in my life's walk, and the depth of my experiences helped me value my many growing sources of joy and happiness. Beth and I loved living in our own home, near Oak Ridge rival Boone High, and on many mornings, we ran together. Then, she would go to her job leasing luxury apartments while I worked freelance and on writing projects like a feature-length screenplay about a boy's experience one summer playing baseball and growing up.

In this setting, my inner poet began to shapeshift. The poem below was written a few months after receiving that first historic note from Tom Tilford. Personally, I feel it shows some signs of improved craftsmanship. Your feedback is always most welcome.

THE LITTLE DEVIL

It chills me to death that
the world passes by
like a pinwheel spin
like a fast-blinking eye

never knowing the touch
of a far-seeing boy
who's aspired to shape–
out of life's gifts–more joy?

No; it's more than that, honestly:
life, when it's withered,
must result in some stockpile
of brilliance delivered.

As a cart passed-by doorsteps
and daily I filled it,
some bell softly sank-in
to earth. I have killed it.

I'm nothing; I'm slipping;
I've read but not written;
to sleep does he lead me;
by devil, I'm smitten.

10

Good Poetry

First published: June 4, 2011

I **MAY NEVER BECOME FAMOUS** as a result of a poem I've written. I reluctantly accepted that probability some time ago, but only after mounting great, concentrated efforts designed to place my poetry within well respected literary publications . . . most of which failed.

I've always been a sincere fan of my mother Lila Darnell's direct, powerful, and stylized creative writing. Through my high school and college educations, exchanges with many other colorful and smart friends and family members, and lifelong exposure to magazines, radio, and cable TV broadcasts, I developed a pretty strong sense for good poetry, and where that odd form of writing fits into the world. In my early 20s, I was introduced to the works of Charles Bukowski, who appeared to me as a 360-degree representation of the life of a successful poet . . . and who wrote books I loved instantly, due to them being so human, approachable, funny, well written, and good. My friend Hardy Edwards introduced me to Bukowski's books, and he later made a short film based on his work. That project put me in direct contact with the writer and his publisher, agent, and friend, John Martin. For a couple of years, I sustained irregular contact with both gentlemen, and oddly, in my day-to-day dealings, I was often thinking of my next letter to Buk.

Meanwhile, the parting days of 1993 had me thinking about my own writing in new ways, under these and other influences. As mentioned previously, Tom Tilford at Midwest Poetry Review had recently opened his door to me, and I wanted to write something truly great, and go for the win. I wrote this on December 27.

ETHEREAL STONES

Thank you for finding me again, old spirit.
We have so many furtive longings to take up,
but we so rarely indulge in them. Certainly,
we have earned this dance this evening.

As my oversensitivity reels atop a selfish stoicism,
the emotions play out and spin dizzily,
creating a whirling centrifugal force of wonder,
shame, fear, concern, pity, remorse, rawness.

Individuals endure so much; the spoils of nations,
the dead, rotting cruelty of pride, the falsehood

of trust, the misrepresentations of so many liars.
Liars, right down the line, pointing at one another.

But the victims, mostly, at the late hour, do not seek
to know who's guilty. They are truly bitter, but in
that there is the peace of the wind, the sunshine, the rain,
the occasional sparkle from a bit of something on the
  sidewalk.

We all know what is right, yet we cannot embrace it.
It's gone on for too long now, and no one is capable
of turning the pride; especially not the leaders.
But we're talking of my body and spirit, aren't we?

Plotting this out, I'm fencing myself into an area where
the gate can be clasped shut and stock taken.
The spirit is full of sadness, the body is capable of
continuing on, but not tuning itself into the soul's tone.

In this quietness, as another series of masterful patterns
daisy-chains down the television for the eyes of my love
and the ears of us both, my spirit drapes itself across this,
another screen. My body calls it forth; there is language!

It grows late, but still I can only grasp at the deep need
beckoning me. The shadows of my life grow longer and
more vacuous, and I can't seem to reach the elusive path
where my soul invites me. Another poem; another dream.

Ever since meeting in Alice Wright's Advanced Placement English class during our senior year of high school, my friend Jay Lerew has shared and stoked my enthusiasm for great literature. He remains the only person I know who can recite long passages of A. E. Housman poems, including but certainly not limited to "Terence, This is Stupid Stuff." This common appreciation for fine writing brought us together often over the years to laugh, drink coffee, and share prized literary gems. From 1988 to 1990, my last years at college, Jay and I were roommates. Together we amassed vast book collections, with many acquisitions made for the sole purpose of impressing each other and our friends. Between us, I'd say we completed a decent pass of classic and contemporary literature. When Hardy introduced Bukowski to me, Jay and several more friends also got hooked right away.

After writing the poem above, I don't recall how quickly I sent it off to Tom at MPR, but I'm pretty sure it was only a matter of hours. But even before doing that, I showed it to Jay. To me, his response is an excellent testament to his friendship, although I also like to attribute it to his great taste in literature: He asked me for a signed copy, and told me he intended to frame it and hang it on his wall.

My wish for you is to have FRIENDS such as this!

In March, 1994, Hardy sent me the news reporting on Bukowski's death. I wrote the poem below in June. The November issue of MPR carried "Ethereal Stones," representing a personal triumph for yours truly. God bless you Tom Tilford . . . and that goes for you, too, Mr. Bukowski, Mr. Martin, Mr. and Mrs. Darnells, Mrs. Wright, Mr. Lerew,

and Mr. Edwards. I thank you all—and many others—from
the bottom of my heart for all the inspiration.

BUK

Bukowski died about two months ago.
The thing about it
was there was nothing to do.

A Bukowski tribute poem?
Like a skateboard for the pope,
only worse.

Nobody that Bukowski loved needed to
hear from me. I well intended to contact
Linda and John Martin, nonetheless.
I still do.

When I heard from Hardy that he'd died
it was so odd because I was building
up to my next Bukowski contact.
Shaping it in my mind.

I was going to tell him I'd finally had
a poem accepted —and here it was.

It struck me that he probably would have
been ready to die after receiving such news from me.

But I had this sense that he liked me because
I'd touched him. He certainly touched me.
Blessed dirty old man; I loved you.   6/2/94

Rewrites

First published: July 16, 2011

THANK YOU VERY MUCH for your interest in this thread, and my ongoing adventures as a poet. This project revisits the experiences of the past 20 years for posterity, your entertainment, and hopefully some enlightenment as well. This is part 11, and number 15 is the last entry I have outlined. In finishing the series up over the next several weeks, I have a few more stories I hope you'll enjoy. The following lines are from "An Essay on Man" published by Alexander Pope in 1734.

> *All Nature is but Art, unknown to thee;*
> *All chance, direction, which thou canst not see;*
> *All discord, harmony not understood;*
> *All partial evil, universal good:*
> *And, spite of pride in erring reason's spite,*
> *One truth is clear, whatever is, is right.*

Out of necessity, the lion's share of my summer 1994 professional effort was dedicated to fulfilling what I had clearly identified as my primary objective: "Get the check." When my poem finally appeared in the October issue of Midwest Poetry Review, it had no real impact in my world, financially or otherwise. I fully intended to keep submitting what I considered to be my best writing to literary magazines and contests, but I had to focus my endeavors more productively to help Beth pay our mortgage and fund our expeditions as tourists and nature-lovers.

In those days, I was growing in capabilities and reputation as a screen and script writer, a trade media journalist, a film, TV, and video production pro, and a sort of marketing and high-tech whiz kid. On July 5, I received a big break: I was hired by BBK Productions to work as the writers' assistant on their pilot for an hour-long dramatic series for Columbia TriStar Pictures. One good thing led to the next; the series was picked-up by then-fledgling Fox television network, and throughout that fall, I worked with an amazing crew as 13 episodes of "Fortune Hunter" came to life, featuring rising star Mark Frankel and a stunning list of Hollywood talents. This poem was written that August.

SATURDAY MORNING, AGE 28

film scheduling, scripts
friendly smiling caring people
making a TV show at network level
that's funny, aspires to and achieves quality

music is lengthening its shadow
swilling a promising luminance
fingers tinkling atop the ivories
harmonies released at last

oh my aunts and uncles
the older friends of my parents
my grandparents my parents my siblings
dear friends dear strangers

every being exists for a purpose
recognized, taunted, lost, sold, claimed
taken for granted, lived to the fullest
it's up to you and me my friends

When "Fortune Hunter" ended, I picked up other contract work, like writing news releases related to the production and post-production industries, writing a feature story for a national trade magazine, and handling script revisions for more TV productions.

On those days not timed on others' clocks, I worked on things like my own business and marketing plans, and pursuing options on literary properties of personal interest. On nights when Beth turned in early, I read, wrote, and searched my soul, ultimately finding that my desire to see my creative writing in literary publications still burned brightly. With 1994 winding down, I mailed polished packages to The Atlanta Review, Sounds of the Street, Hellas, Literal Latte, Pebbles, Poetry Motel, Stone Shoes, Good Housekeeping, The

Southern Review, and The Paris Review, and a few manuscript contests I hoped to win.

The new year soon pulled me back into financial distress and the frenzy of Orlando's freelance marketplace. Chasing the dollar, I had excellent company, and terrific good fortune in running mates. Then and now, few in Central Florida have been as successful as independent producer and director of photography Randy Baker, who took me under his wing as a collaborator and showed me what is possible with diligence, hard work, perseverance, and charm. Between the freelance production activities Randy offered and the writing-related contracts mentioned above (many of which involved him integrally), I achieved some financial stability even without having a full-time job.

Reaching that new plateau, I reassessed the sum total of my professional achievements with the goal of focusing-in properly . . . and happily, I began to pinpoint some opportunities. This is from a strategic marketing plan I put together in February, 1995.

"Since every professional needs to maximize their internal and external communications and their existing inventory of rights, a specialist in industry marketing who can create strategic communications tools quickly is extremely valuable."

Also: *"A crucial aspect of future success is increased recognition through legitimate literary channels."*

With a growing sense of my unique value propositions and my marketing imperatives, I continued pursuing what came my way while reaching for more whenever possible.

Looking back, it's plain to see that most of my extracurricular efforts missed their primary marks, as the rejection slips steadily arrived in the mail each week, constantly reminding me of my lack of merit and unimportance as a writer, from the perspectives of so many editors and literary gatekeepers.

Fortunately, I had some other heavy hitters in my corner. If you have followed along in my narrative, you've seen how important my brother has always been in my life, and how my own being has often taken a backseat to his, from my point of view. That may sound convoluted, but if you have read "Wordsworth," I expect you will understand my meaning.

On March 3, I received the fax transmittal from Scott shown on the next page.

Without a doubt, receiving his feedback gave me a giant swell of pride and confidence. Later that month, I received a letter from a dear friend of my mother named Gay Henderson. After Scott's diving accident in 1991, Mom had gotten us all involved with a support group for spinal injured individuals and their families in Orlando. It was an eye- and mind-opening experience to say the least, meeting young men and women who had suffered spinal injuries but moved back into life so normally that it was very reassuring. Dr. John Ross-Duggan was one of the inspirational wheelchair-bound individuals we met there. Gay was John's mother, and after meeting her through the support group, she and my mom had formed a solid friendship. Through wonderful, long, typewritten letters that Mom often shared with me, Gay dazzled us with scenarios right out of the movies like "84 Charing Cross Road" and "Out of Africa." I only wish we'd had the chance to get to know her and her husband Allyn better; sadly, Gay passed away in August, 1996.

Facsimile Cover Sheet

To: Roger K. Darnell
Company: Darnell Works
Phone: 407-649-8626
Fax: 407-649-8626

From: Scott A. Darnell
Company:
Phone: 813-465-2148
Fax: 813-465-2148

Date: 03/03/95
Pages including this
cover page:

Comments:

Broham.

I'm impressed. Perhaps one of the greatest wonders of the paralyzed world is whether or not outsiders can understand our situation and to what degree. Every move or decision we make brings on the feeling of scrutiny by others, which is a much higher version of that from our previous life. What might seem dictated to our situation now might be completely different from the previous, but usually not taken into consideration. Also, granted, we give very little latitude as to giving credit to the outside world for what they are capable of grasping. Perhaps we NEED to be the only one aware of our own private hell. Being it's master gives us strength. Regardless, it is hard to appreciate that the small mole hills we conquer could mean much to others in this world of great accomplishment. Your story taught me that you have absorbed and might understand my situation more than I have given you credit for. I apologize for that, and would like to thank you for having done so. I love you Roo.

The Other Broham.

The fax from my brother and Gay's letter remain among the greatest achievements I've earned through writing. Together, they provided some magic which, along with my experiences, has worked to transform my thinking on the subject of literary fame over time. Through the words of Scott and Gay, I saw that my writing had already connected me very deeply and profoundly with my brother, my mother, and one of the wisest and most wonderful people I had met in the world.

218 Via Graziana
Newport Beach, California 92663
March 23, 1995

Roger dear,

    You might not remember me, but I have had the joy of a running correspondence with your Mother for about three years now, and it's been a very enriching friendship.

    BUT her latest share with me has been a copy of your WORDSWORTH!!!!!! I've read it slowly four times, and each time it gets even better!!! It's without a doubt the most sensitive, visually artistic piece of literature I've read in years . That you have captured the essence of paralysis of the body while maintaining such a fevered brilliance of the mind is the focus. Do you suppose it is true that if you lose your sight, your hearing intensifies? And if this is so, think of all the intensities that grow after paralysis! You have!

    Please make the effort to have this published so others may enjoy it, too. I feel very very privileged.

    Give my best to Beth. How was your video work in the Bahamas? Allyn and I just got back from a very energetic trip to Chile's lake district and out to Easter Island to investigate those mysterious "moai" that dot that rounded lava landscape. The closest island to Easter is Pitcairn, some 2200 miles further on! So one can easily accept that the first inhabitants were survivors of very long sails. I was surprised that our guide to these mysteries -- a man from Pitcairn with the usual name of "Christian" (as in Mutiny on the Bounty)-- feels Thor Heyerdahl is an arrogant liar! So, having read AKU AKU in prep. for this trip, I now have to dissuade myself from his theories.

    Anyway....keep this passion alive in your writing, Roger. I think you and your whole family have tons of talent!

        All the best,

        Gay

Also, I was already very aware of having built those connections without "publication," and Gay's encouragement led to a great deal more outreach on my part over the years aimed at getting "Wordsworth" into print. It did generate several warm responses from respected editors . . . but it has been brought to the public only through this project you're reading. By publishing it here, I've honored Gay's request, and that's just one of many reasons I'm very proud to honor this poet's arc. Through this self-chosen adventure I set out on long ago, with support from my wife and many other friends and family members, I have found my talents and my career. Along the way, I've also earned the respect and admiration of many great people . . . some of whom I know are real fans of my writing.

Cheers!

12

Resistance

First published: July 23, 2011

IN THE SPRING OF 1995, I was trying to be many things to many people, and those wide attempts to stretch, please and succeed consumed so much energy that more than once, I was caught unprepared for the results. Especially for my inner-poet, it was a mad time.

That January, I had sent the following letter to Tom Tilford at Midwest Poetry Review to thank him for publishing Ethereal Stones, share more work and continue building our relationship:

Roger Darnell
211 East Esther Street
Orlando, FL 32806-3018
407 / 649 / 8626

January 13, 1995

Midwest Poetry Review
Box 4776
Rock Island, IL 61201

Dear Tom:

Happy new year. I hope you're well.

Since our last exchange around this time last year, and since receiving the 10/94 issue of MPR, you've occupied many of my thoughts. First, I want to thank you for publishing Ethereal Stones. The strokes were all there on the page. I shall always be extremely grateful for that, Tom.

Opposite E.S. is Rose-Glass Medallion -- a polished vision from Sean Brendan-Brown in Iowa. Elsewhere, Gregory V. Driscoll's Night Vision yanks me into a dream, and Robert C. Hornbuckle seizes my senses in The Silence of Deep Cold.

Though I could easily get carried away with this, Sharon W. Flynn's Muskrat Dreams and Mary Kraft's Death-Wish reflect something I've gathered from your correspondence: poetry's colorful road to hope. A positive, sound, extrasensory melody sings through your publication -- your community's pulsing oversoul.

Sheila Desmond's Mother and Daughter chimes to me, Judith Cunningham's The Garden stops the wind, Nicolas Pastrone's Seventeen takes me *there*, and Kristine E. Meredith's Childhood Storm and William Sowell's Oh, To Be Young Again -- plus so many others -- speak my language.

I anxiously await the next performance of the MPR choir.

Meanwhile, events have kept me far removed from your deadlines, and I'm unsure of any current topics. So I'm just sending something wonderful. Hope you enjoy them.

Best wishes,

Roger Darnell

3 Poems: My Cluttered Table; What would it take to make this a good night?; Seagulls
Bio (--FYI--)

P.S. Your Comment on WCW fascinates me. It's helped me understand the doctor much better. Are you familiar with Kenneth Koch's Variations on a Theme...? It splits my sides!

Here's the sticky note he returned with my letter.

When April came, I had more poetry to share with Tom. Into my care package I optimistically added The Gondoliers Sing Love Songs, which as you may recall, had its world premiere in part two of this series. The response came by postal mail; dated on my 29th birthday, it appeared soon thereafter in my Esther Street mailbox. Much to my surprise, it was not from Tom at all . . . but rather, John K. Ottley, Jr., the magazine's new publisher.

Since receiving his letter so many years ago, I have found that Mr. Ottley is a very accomplished poet and publisher in his own right. He was quite personal with me right away; the volume and depth of his correspondence really had my head swimming. At first, I was very flattered to have anyone provide specific comments on poems I'd written—so naturally, hearing them from the new publisher of a magazine I'd come to cherish, my attention was undivided . . . and I was literally living a dream. Unfortunately, by the time I got to the bottom, I was fuming. I wrote him back immediately, telling him to remove my poem from consideration.

I do not have the letter I sent to Mr. Ottley, but his reply dated May 19 indicates how little time passed between our respective snail-mailings—and the general spirit of my missive, for whatever that may be worth.

This entry contains no poems. Rather, I will just end with my follow-up response to Mr. Ottley. To all of this, I'll add that the experience has been instrumental in my education as an aspiring poet, as a writer and as a professional. Among those I consider to be gateways into the literary world, I feel very lucky to have met both Tom Tilford and John K. Ottley, Jr.

What would have happened if Gondoliers had appeared in the July 1995 issue of Midwest Poetry Review? It would have been great, for sure; I can't imagine how things may have proceeded from there, if only I'd been better at dealing with Mr. Ottley's quirkiness, and his straightforward criticism. The man took an interest in me and really seemed intent on publishing my work; for those honors, I remain humbled and extremely grateful.

As my journey has continued, I've always tried to value any input received from anyone I respect, even if we disagree. I know that openness and willingness to bend is critical for achieving things with others . . . and that, with a little help, anything really is possible.

May 16, 1995

John Ottley, Jr.
Midwest Poetry Review
Box 20236
Atlanta, GA 30325-0236

Dear John:

Thanks for the letter. I honor your right to reply and appreciate your following through with me. That you are opening up your hopper is important to note; that I so brashly assumed you'd continue the previous policy as I did is humbling. I apologize for mistaking your judgment along those lines.

Meanwhile, I will also echo the sentiment that prompted my last letter: I sincerely wish you'd stick to the point and concentrate on communicating your message.

Your clean letters consist of terse paragraphs with no typos. Your presence in them is respectable. Your humor is also appreciated. However, I do believe some of the words you've chosen to send my way have undermined your messages.

For example, a tad more consideration might have led to your finding another way to relate the act of returning my poem to pulling a log from a woodpile and continuing to describe how others tumble down to fill the space. To me, that doesn't indicate much respect for the work or the folks behind it, especially since you said it to me (a writer). Also you tell me you look for poems which hold themselves together despite the form. The way I think, rhyming poetry excels by virtue of the form, which many ignore or otherwise don't take the time to understand. Although I realize you can't get inside every person's head, what I'm saying is that you can make choices which would endear me (a writer) more toward you (a publisher).

I'll elaborate a bit more. To be real honest, I sense a contemptuous tone throughout your last letter, right up until you wish me the best, bro, and sign 'yours sincerely' (GULP). Since that's your closing, I do thank you for the warm sentiments. If I haven't imagined it, the leer must be unintended.

To help you see my perspective, I've so far written four screenplays for feature films (two written for-hire), an original half-hour teleplay currently under consideration by Toronto's ShowCase Television, a dozen short film scripts (half have been produced), many commercials, PSAs, marketing scripts, articles in prominent national film, TV, pro sound and recording industry trade magazines and volumes of creative work. Over eight years of production work, I've helped produce presentations for top film industry executives and recently participated in productions on pilots and episodes for Columbia Pictures TV.

Thanks again for your sincerity, for relating what issues did come across loudly and clearly in your letters (you did like my work, you're at the helm publishing a new MPR, that you take a personal interest in poetry), and for sticking with me as I try to help you make the most of the opportunity you're shaping.

Best wishes,
(signed)
Roger Darnell

13

Fame and Fortune

First published: August 13, 2011

A **GOOD NUMBER OF GREAT PEOPLE** have expressed appreciation for my writing over the years. Since long ago, many believers have endorsed these abilities, and I feel that their belief is essential to who I am. When I think about what's to come for me as a writer and artist, I'm inspired by the idea of honoring each of those individuals, and all others interested in my words. Gratefully, I'll carry on.

In the summer of 1995, I joined the production crew of the primetime NBC television series "seaQuest" at Universal Studios Florida, and began an adventure I'll never forget, helping produce 13 episodes with a Who's Who of spectacular production and entertainment industry talents. We were in Orlando, making headlines in all the top national trades well before the first episode of "SeaQuest 2032" hit the airwaves featuring Michael Ironside, Roy Scheider, Michael York, and scores of other hot and rising Hollywood stars.

I earned my job from the prolific television producer and director Steve Beers, by committing to handling script distribution and revisions for all the producers and writers, just as I'd done for him and the other producers on "Fortune Hunter" the previous year. That show for Fox had made a big splash and also involved serious heavy hitters, but seaQuest was a phenomenon . . . a massive franchise for NBC, Amblin Television, Universal Television, and all the other industry All-Stars involved.

Engaged as the one and only "Assistant to the Producers, Florida" for production during the series' third season, I interfaced directly with every person listed in the credits for each of these hour-long episodes, and many others at the networks, post-production companies, area film commissions, attractions, restaurants, golf resorts, and beyond. Along with Mr. Beers, executive producers Patrick Hasburgh and Clifton Campbell were my top bosses, and Michael Ironside also joined them in taking me under their wings. Suddenly, Beth and I were part of the bona fide entertainment industry.

During the weeks of September, October and November, our show made waves across America and beyond, and when we learned that seaQuest would not be renewed, along with legions of others, the full cast and crew united in grief. We wrapped that December and went our separate ways. Most of those people I have not seen nor heard from for 15 years, but I have had some colorful exchanges with a few, including recently crossing paths with Anson Williams of Happy Days fame, who masterfully directed three seaQuest episodes that season.

During the seaQuest production, I was normally on-the-run as a subservient worker bee handling my varied chores. My industriousness caught Ironside's attention right away, and he enlisted me on a few of his personal missions. A fellow writer, he quickly sensed my aspirations, and in him, I found an extraordinary role model, and a good friend. Patrick also afforded me a ton of unforgettable experiences, and by shooting straight with me and being my hero, he truly inspired me. Everywhere I turned during the seaQuest experience, something new and unbelievable happened . . . like having a conversation with Dom DeLuise, who shook my hand after meeting me and made a lovely scene for me:

Roger Darnell. ROGER DARNELL! What a great name!

In contrast, my progression as a poet during the same era was completely forgettable. The Summer 1995 issue of 24-7 Artzine carried my poem "John Wayne Dies Again" accompanied by an odd and striking illustration of a tied-up, skeletal cowboy being tormented by a nude female specter. As I continued my correspondence with the editor, he never was able to spell my name right.

Although my other exchanges with literary editors led nowhere, I still found inspiration in my growing gallery of experiences, and wrote some memorable poetry. Before seaQuest was canceled, I also seized the chance to write a spec episode, in the hope that it might get produced in the fourth season. My script was read and discussed at length, and Ironside offered to work with me on it if season four came to pass. As you can imagine, following my investments of so much effort and hope, the show's demise crushed me.

In early November I learned I had maybe a month left on the show, so as the weeks rolled along, I started searching for projects, and putting out word that I'd soon be available. Here's something I wrote late in the evening of November 15.

> not sleepy time
> for a creeping gnaw
> outside my mind
> trying the walls
>
> in between now
> it slams and echoes
> anything is game
> any progress
>
> guards in rotation
> miss the assault
> through it crashes
> stealthy, hungry
>
> unseen coming
> all upon us
> it's your winner
> claimed its prize

The year to follow was highlighted by a lot of fun freelance production and writing adventures, along with much more devotion to personal screenwriting projects and creative writing submissions. In the early days of 1997, I put the finishing touches on my sixth feature film screenplay, adding it to my shelf of unpublished manuscripts beside my spec seaQuest episode, two poetry collections, and a growing volume of short dramatic scripts, stories, and journals.

Lightning struck for me again that February when producer extraordinaire John Melfi hired me to serve as script coordinator during production of HBO's historic, award-winning miniseries "From the Earth to the Moon." To my shock and delight, when I was shown to my office in Bungalow 3 at the Disney-MGM Studios, it was the exact same office I'd left back on my birthday in 1992 after working on "Flipper."

My second tour of duty in that tiny room remains one of the most awesome highlights of my life. The illustrious writer-producer-director Graham Yost came to be a close friend and mentor then, and I also met and collaborated with Tom Hanks, Ron Howard, Lili Zanuck, Frank Marshall, Jon Turteltaub, David Frankel, Sally Field, Jonathan Mostow, Tony To, NASA astronauts Dave Scott and Buzz Aldrin, many of the world's finest actors, and countless other remarkable and sterling human beings, on a momentous, once-in-a-lifetime project.

Beth and I had ridden enough waves by then to recognize HBO's project as a tsunami-sized opportunity, and at the end of 1997, we packed up and moved to Los Angeles, with great expectations. January 1, 1998, was the first day of our westward relocation, and three and a half years later, we were "expecting" a baby girl, and we celebrated our ninth wedding anniversary with some other family members on a ski trip to Lake Tahoe. Soon thereafter, we packed up again and moved back East, this time, to the mountains of North Carolina. Within two months, we became parents, finally realizing who we'd been missing: Amelia, and many other family members and friends . . . eventually including Amelia's little brother Riley.

Before we moved to California, at a film industry party in Orlando, I ran into a friend named Tom Oakes who described what happens when a person moves to LA.

> *Whatever it is that you **DO**, you realize that, and you go where they hire those people, and it's like you get a ticket with a number on it. Eventually your number's called, and then you either go to the top or you get shot out and you have to start all over again.*

I never forgot Tom's scenario as I plugged away in LA hoping that my number would soon be called. Month after month I wondered, would my opportunity come as a screenwriter, a writer's assistant, a producer, a poet, a director? No indeed; as a marketer and public relations executive, I was eventually able to land a job (after five excruciating months), and then begin to flourish. From there, my career progressed back to the point where in May of 2000, I launched The Darnell Works Agency as my private consultancy.

Beth and I were really having a blast, living a lifestyle that was all us, and growing together as grown-ups very nicely. Although we weren't rich by LA standards, we were conscious of our great fortune. One evening as we walked in the hills of our "Shermancino" neighborhood, we envisioned raising the children we were hoping for alongside cousins, aunts, uncles, and grandparents in Boone. Then we put the wheels in motion and relocated lock, stock, and barrel to a place we had only visited on vacation, joining many others in Beth's family as residents. Amelia's birthday in August is an annual reminder of our tenure here.

Across each of these various phases and settings, writing has helped me to achieve focus, define my personal balance, and pursue it. I wrote some more screenplays over the years, and put some effort into the idea of launching my career as a filmmaker . . . all of which only left a little room for poetry. My experience on seaQuest led me to feel that I could become successful as a screenwriter if I could just find the right project at the right time, and give it my best shot. While I had done okay as a video scriptwriter in Orlando and I did land agency representation during our time in Hollywood, despite my best efforts, I received no screenplay bites, nor screenwriting offers. When we left, I just decided to keep looking for the right opportunities, knowing I would need to write scripts on spec for anything I wanted to pursue. Meanwhile, I put my primary focus on being truly great as a business partner to my clients, and as a husband and father.

There have been a few interesting screen project developments over the recent years, including some that may yet play out dramatically. Of course, the poet has continued toiling away in the margins of my busy, happy, relatively well-balanced existence, so there is still more to share in this series.

For a year and a half after Amelia was born, I wrestled at night with a poetic tribute to her arrival. Up to that point, I think poetry had been something different to me; facing the weight of writing an ode to our miraculous first child, I finally signed-off on the epic wordplay I am proud to share with you below. I hope you enjoy it.

AMELIA'S BIRTHDAY POEM

Waking up at a total loss
For where I was . . . slowly came awake.
Day had begun, I told myself,
Quite unaware of the day's high stake.

John O'Groats, right on Pico Ave.,
I ate with Ted—a nice breakfast spot.
LA was totally soaking in –
I'd had good times these two days, I thought.

Morning meeting at The Village failed
To gel—although it was cool to tour.
Walking into KLCS,
Friend Brenda's jaw nearly hit the floor.

Flying, racing up freeway ramps,
My Sebring—burgundy—made it fun
Prowling into parking lots
At Staples Center—or in the sun.

SIGGRAPH clogged all convention halls;
I searched my way through them for discreet.
Angus met me by chance—by fate?
I wonder, watching the scenes repeat.

Passing badge off to Ted in show's
High-def HQ, the time dawned on me;
Wending way back to Sebring's space
I panicked over how late I'd be!

LAX isn't very close
To where I sat at fifteen 'til two.
Getting onto that plane at three
Absorbed my thoughts; worried, off I flew.

Knifing back to the rental drop
I didn't make any driving friends.
Pulling in—there were scores of cars
Awaiting checkers to check them in!

Glancing down at my watch again
I saw I'd thirty-nine minutes more;
Giving up, just about, I saw
The checker wave me on through his door.

On the shuttle bus, wondered why
I'd been so panicked about the flight;
I might miss it, I had no doubt,
But if I did, it was still all right.

Only twenty more minutes stood
Until my flight would be underway.
Stepping into the Delta line,
A supervisor's help saved the day.

In my seat, calm, onboard the plane,
I called my wife just to let her know.
What a relief, we laughed aloud,
And counted hours still left to go.

Though I spoke with a gentleman
Across America, with no break,
Names are absent from memories.
He made me laugh; helped me stay awake.

Also, checking by cell phone from
Atlanta, Beth and I spoke of him.
Sounding sleepy, relaxed, and fine,
The LA trip seemed a winning whim.

Seated for the trip's last flight,
Another guy landed in my row,
We just talked the whole trip away.
His name? It slipped my mind, too, you know?

Back in Greensboro right at one,
I walked alone through the parking lot.
Aimed for home, our Acord woke up;
I paid for parking . . . and out we shot.

Blackness paved all the space around
The road, I found, as I made my way.
Skirting Winston and Salem fast,
The darkness stuck to this brand new day.

Music carried me over roads
That turned and rose inside ink-thick mists.
Lights showed up in the rearview, too,
To heighten drama of highway's twists.

LA, distant by now, it seemed
A glowing gem in my darkened mind.
Feeling thrilled to have slipped away ...
A victory of a sacred kind.

Climbing finally past Deep Gap,
I knew I'd sleep in my bed that night;
Knew I'd witness my daughter's birth;
I knew that things would now be all right.

Driving back across Boone, alone,
It felt so great to be almost there.
Turns led straight back to Rocky Creek;
I got the mail—and inhaled the air!

Windows fell as I rolled by creek,
So joyous journey was ending here.
Fifty-eight after two a.m.,
I felt a tickle inside my car.

Nearly home—the darn cell phone rang!
I answered, "Hello?" "Where are you?" came
Beth. I told her, "Almost there." "Good,
My water broke." I forgot my name ...

Also everything else just then.
"We need to go to Lenoir right now."
Swerving, missing the tree ahead,
I gulped, "I'm almost there. Coming!" (Wow!)

Beth had spent the last hour or more
Preparing us by arranging gear,
Packing truck with our babe supplies,
And pressing phone, dialed-out, to ear.

Calls to Delta confirmed my plane,
She'd just not gotten me through my phone,
So she kept on arranging stuff
And calling, otherwise here alone.

Ann and Chuck—also Grace and Claire –
Were with our grandfolks Dan and Lil,
In Wisconsin there, don't you know?
My wife alone sat upon our hill.

Calmly, doing all she could do,
She thus stood by . . . or she paced around.
Though contractions she did not feel,
She knew our time was still counting down.

Bradley Method's the class we took
Through Julie; made us a birthing plan!
At the time—about three fifteen –
That plan was how I was able to stand,

Move around, gather up some things
With real and practical use and get
Them and me buckled into truck –
Plus Beth's composure, I can't forget.

Soon enough, we were on our way
On down the mountain—back on the road!
Caldwell's hospital beckoned us . . .
Through thirty miles more of twists we rode.

Time slipped by on that early morn,
We made our way through the misty dark.
Deer were walking along the road
That led, at last, to our place to park.

Weeks before we had toured the floor
Of Caldwell Hospital's birthing ward;
Who'd have thought we'd arrive so soon?
Though Beth was sleepy, excitement soared.

Still, her water had broken, but
She wasn't feeling contractions strong.
Settling into our room we got
To hear Amelia's soft heartbeat song.

Learning from the admitting nurse
She wasn't dilated much by then,
Beth prepared for a long, tough bout . . .
And wished she'd feel the real pains begin.

Roger Darnell   **87**

Julie's class once more gave me fuel;
We started walking around the floor.
Timing pains as the minutes passed
Until, at last, I could go no more.

Sleep demanded I soon relent—
I made my bed in the sleeper chair.
Beth walked on as I sank to sleep;
My dreams were like some surreal nightmare.

Hearing voices, I stirred awake.
A hand extended my way and shook;
Dr. Yun was a nice young guy,
I noticed, watching the care he took

Speaking gently as ultra sound
Scanned Beth. Imagine the shock we felt
Seeing what he then found: "The head."
Our expectations, just then, did melt.

For, you see, this position's called
A breech, and even in that spent state,
Quickly senses became awake—
I found my feet and rejoined my mate.

Holding hands, we heard Dr. Yun
Explain that really we had no choice—
Beth would feel, he assured, no pain—
And soon we'd hear our Amelia's voice.

Having never expected this
It felt as though our whole world was gone;
This was our "worst scenario"—
At least that's what our first thoughts were on.

Doctors came, midwives, nurses, too—
The operation room was abuzz.
Beth was wheeled in, then given meds,
While I scrubbed up like a doctor does.

Somewhere through these activities,
I think we saw things would be okay.
Fate had thrown us an awesome curve—
But still, it was our Amelia's day!

All the staff were true gifts from God—
We couldn't want more or better care.
Bets were off on the costs we'd face—
And yet, we counted our blessings there.

When I walked into surgery,
I saw Beth's face—and she looked quite calm.
Coming near, she looked up at me—
Just on the verge of becoming Mom.

"This is just so surreal," she said—
I laughed—and peered up and over drape
Right there—out came our baby then—
With cord wrapped twice round her neck, like tape.

Then our grumpy newborn was brought
Where we could see, at last: What a sight!
All we'd done as a couple had
Paid off: Amelia May was all right.

Then they asked me to bring our girl
Toward the nursery right away.
Beth said "go," so off we went:
Me, in my scrubs, and Amelia May.

Hitting the doors, I saw Ginny there,
Her gaze was full on the little one.
"That the Darnell girl?" came her voice—
"It is," I said, to recognition none.

"I'm the Grandma," she proudly said,
Just focused in on her third grandkid.
"I'm the Dad," I then gushed her way,
At last she saw me—and laugh we did.

In the nursery, some tests were run,
It broke me in on a lot to come:
Nurses poked, then they prodded more,
I stared them down, feeling mad and dumb.

Ginny helped so by being there;
Her fingertip in Amelia's hand
Made her granddaughter lots more calm,
And, for her son-in-law, helped him stand.

Seizing moment, I hit our room,
And called my mom to give her our news.
She was shocked—but stuck to her plans,
And said she'd leave after that night's snooze.

After calling my other folks,
I aimed the camera—improv time!
Documenting Amelia's birth
Though in my plans—had not been divine.

Sorta scary my form appears
Within that videotaped report,
Trying gracefully to announce
Our daughter's here—and she's fine, in short . . . .

Taping that, back to nursery
I ran, with camera in my hand,
Through the glass I was motioned back
Inside—and there with Grandma, scanned.

So upset, but so quick to calm,
Our little one had her video shot.
Now shaking less, she tried to look,
But clearly, cycdrops used hurt a lot.

At this time, while we stood in watch,
Our Beth was wheeled back into our suite.
Soon I went back to let her know
These tests would soon all be done/complete.

Roger Darnell

Now is when our nurse Crystal comes
To mind—amazing the care she gave,
From delivery room until
We left; so kind, calming, strong, and sage.

Footage tells the full story here:
When Crystal pushed our new baby through
Doorway into our room to give,
At last, the mother her babe, I knew

Something special had blessed this day.
My wife just bawled for a bit before
Crystal managed to pass across
The baby—then she just cried some more.

Nothing ever will ever touch
That perfect happiness; like a toy
We'd loved and lost—but then found again;
The definition of overjoy.

Grandma Ginny and Grandpa Bill
Made sure that mother and babe were fine,
Then they headed home, giving us
Darnells some make-new-acquaintance time.

Crystal also was there to make
Us very comfy, so blessed we were
Then and there. When the girls kicked back,
I forced a move off my derriere.

Beth was hip to my getaway
For rest—and then to send email out
Sharing news of our baby girl.
I kissed them both, then I headed out.

Being honest, that drive is not
A memory I can recollect;
Getting home on that afternoon,
Emotions hit I did not expect.

After showering, I'd unpacked,
Was stretching out for a few hours' nap,
Thinking then about Beth and child,
Was overwhelmed with a sobbing snap.

Found the phone and then called my wife,
Related missing her, being sick,
Gushing pride in our child and her,
plus saying, "Know I'll be back real quick."

Sleep was quickly upon me then,
Arriving fast . . . as night seized the day.
Soon, a stirring of things to do
Awoke and put me upon my way.

First, to office to pull some still
JPEGs from video footage shot,
Post them onto the web and write
A note announcing news on our tot.

Emails went out at half-past eight:
I sent out sixty, all still archived,
Quite triumphantly telling all
Amelia May had today arrived.

Also, pointing them to the site
To see first shots of her and request
Birthday messages back from them,
To show our girl how she's truly blessed.

Packing up, grabbed my laptop, then
I loaded up and took off again.
Super tired-out and mostly wrecked,
My mind was teeming with spirit kin.

I had triggered a lot of vibes
In sending all of those emails out;
Uncle Scott, had been spreading word
All day and night, too, as I found out.

Granny Bea, Uncle Charlie, John,
Aunt Dean, my Grandpas, other uncles, aunts,
Friends and cousins who passed away
Were all in mind in a joyful dance.

Tears were running, but on I drove,
The road in darkness and fog obscured;
Lucky me, a car's taillights showed
My path to steer . . . and so, reassured.

After passing that highway's worst,
Arriving into Lenoir's town light,
Guiding taillights just disappeared;
I'm sure my shepherds were there that night.

Somewhere during that drive I thought
Of this—a poem on Amelia's day . . .
Starting out with me, unaware,
And ending in such a special way.

Beth was holding her, swaddled tight,
At nine fifteen, when I made it back.
Nothing possibly could have made
Me any happier than seeing that.

Hugs and kisses so freely flowed . . .
I laid in bed with them, holding tight.
Telling Beth of the pictures sent,
I got my laptop and showed the site.

Then, the emails began to hit,
And I, again, was just overwrought.
My experience was no help
In dealing with those outpoured thoughts.

Reading notes from my mom, and Bart,
Lemays, Miss Cleff, then the Bakers and more,
Rendered speechless this normal ham,
I balled and blubbered as never before.

Soon, composure was all around,
Until a nurse came to take the girl;
Seeking to bathe her, then weigh her in,
Our flat refusal made that nurse's hair curl.

Online love kept on pouring in,
We relished words from the Jenners plus
Zobrists . . . then Uncle Tommy's laughs
And Uncle Scott's note were priceless to us.

August 16 would see us there,
In learning mode on so many things:
Nursing, dealing with Beth's vast pain,
the baby's choking and Martha's "wings" . . .

Gramma Lila's arrival, too,
At end of day, when we'd all head for
Temporary place we then called home
'Til ours was done: Ann and Chuck's ground floor.

That night, too, Ann and Chuck would meet
Their niece . . . but since this poem's about
Birthday girls' very first day, we'll stop
When lights in room 366 went out.

14

Ramblings

First published: August 27, 2011

MORE THAN TEN YEARS AGO, after relocating to the Blue Ridge Mountains and making final preparations for parenthood (including studying The Bradley Method), Beth and I launched into this current phase of our love story. Experiencing life's joys and sorrows together over the next couple of years, while diligently tending to my business and supporting personal projects for many members of the family, I wondered what was to come for the creative writer. In 2002, I made up an answer, in the form of a new writing project named Ramble. In it, I aimed to address my personal challenges, write simply, and seek new focus. From the beginning, these words have appeared at the top: "This document will hopefully grow in the weeks ahead to represent a journey: the rediscovery of the writer inside a person caught up in his life as businessman, husband, and parent."

Going mostly on instinct, I limited each line to 40 characters, wrote the first entry 73 lines long, and planned to make each subsequent verse one line shorter. If all went as hoped, I figured the final, single-line entry would be something significant, even if most of the others might be less memorable.

Leaping ahead to the present, Ramble has been somewhat miraculous to me; as you might expect, it changed dramatically over time . . . and so have I. For the first, longest verses, I vented in detail about momentous developments, including some of the bigger political and global issues of those days. Progressively, I grew more and more daunted in facing the need to communicate things of real importance concisely. For anyone arriving at a crossroads in life with ability and time to write, I encourage a similar writing challenge. If you don't have years and years to devote, begin with a five-line poem, then count down four, three, two and one: In my experience, it's a productive approach at focusing oneself.

My personal website did not exist when I started writing Ramble, but it features all the most recent entries. Since writing number 17 in early 2008 and publishing it there the next day, I've written seven others that I've instantly published. One year ago, I wrote and added #6 in honor of our son Riley.

Hoping your interest runs deeper, I'm proud to share a few of my favorite rambles. They span from the project's earliest days through until now, almost; #5 was written in March, 2011. Below, all make their debut. The very next chapter of Arc of the Poet will end this tale, while also seeing

Ramble through to its finale. I appreciate your interest immensely, and hope you will stay tuned, keep in touch, and enjoy everything life has to offer.

#70 (2002)

So, on a weekend, what exactly is it
that's keeping me away from tackling
one of these longer-form projects of
personal origination? Not exactly an
easy question to answer, but I do
realize that the key to "jumping" when
I get the opportunity depends upon me
getting through this. My first
reaction is to think about these other
standing items: the next novel from
my step father-in-law; the electronic
books and developments underway for my
father-in-law; the screenplay project
which is certainly a priority at the
moment; and after that, my sort of
aimless, hard to pin-down hesitation
in knowing exactly which project to
"jump" into. If I get that far, there
is certainly one project I think of,
but knowing that I need to be making
daily progress with these other
initiatives—plus of course finding
my third client and landing them—
it's a very sticky cobweb I have to

spin my way through to actually begin
contemplating launching my efforts.
It's easier to pick up a book, do
some straightening in my office, write
my mom or my brother an email, or go
and see what it is that Amelia and her
mother are up to. The ability to
actually focus on that creative work,
to make it absolutely phenomenal, is
a goal I am passionate about for good
reasons: if I pursue it, I want it to
be great, to succeed where my other
completed creative pursuits have not.
I can remember reading about A.E.
Housmann, coming to see that after he
wrote A Shropshire Lad, he essentially
retired from writing poetry. His
powerful words, written before he
reached 25, I believe, touched me very
deeply when I was young, and I was
pretty determined to follow-through on
my poetic pursuits; seeing an end to
the achievements of someone I sought
to emulate at such an early age, I was
troubled as I considered my future.
I've always thought about writing
like my favorite authors, and making
movies like my favorite filmmakers,
and I can see that failing to achieve

something close in any of these areas would be a significant disappointment in my life. So, if I'm to live the life I've aspired to for so long, I need to create every aspect of those successes that are so far immaterial. I'm extremely grateful for the dreams which drive me on; having them is a gift . . . and the more readily I can see them, the better my chances at keeping the fire of determination alive within me. Continuing on at the pace that my wife and I are enjoying, we'll pay off two homes, live a great life, and raise two children with much love and joy; hallelujah! By seizing any chances to write I can put more icing on my cake.

. . .

#67 (2003)

I am writing from a place that has evolved since the beginning of this project, but it's the place that we envisioned prior to relocating here, and I have attained it more than once over these past two years. It is a place of harmony . . . where I can enjoy our beautiful forest surroundings, the peace of trickling waterfalls and the

dazzling brilliance of sunlight sifted
through treetops and reflected from
flat eddies in the creek's shimmering
waters. Even the buzzing of insects
is a joy to behold here, because they
are brilliantly contrasted with those
sounds from locales we have occupied
in the past. I can immerse in this
splendor of nature because my wife and
my daughter are also enjoying harmony
today . . . out at the library or perhaps
playing at a park . . . and our son grows
contentedly inside his mother's womb,
slowly but surely becoming. All along
the journey that has brought us here,
this place has existed, but often it
lies beyond our grasp. Even during
times of peace, some unexplainable
phenomena occupy our energies to the
extent that we pre-conceive some of
the difficulties we might face, or we
puzzle over challenges on the outer
peripheries of our lives. These past
few nights, my wife has dreamt of the
most horrible situations with our
daughter . . . and as I laid sleepless
but exhausted in bed last night, I too
was visited with torturous visions . . .
as if imagining a benign scrape on our

daughter's elbow isn't horrifying in
itself. Such thoughts prompt me, on a
morning like this one, to gaze at my
daughter with such profound love . . . to
realize the limitation of the security
I can offer as she, too, continues to
become. And the blessing that is most
evident is this place, and all that it
means to us in our hearts and minds.
For here, aside from the riches nature
surrounds us with, we are also wealthy
in loving family and the overflowing
fruits of nurturing, wholesome values.
Beauty, fine arts, fun, adventure,
bonds of love, community, and self-
identity are giving our child a unique
and solid perspective in the world,
and she, together with her cousins,
will shepherd our little boy all the
days of his childhood, until he grows
with them into a full human being.
These children, invested with the very
best we have to offer, in a place that
seems as though it will always hold
its magic on its very surface—
a simple empire that knows, respects
and admires them—have every chance
of becoming great. These virtues
kindle my thoughts on this summer day.

. . .

#61 (2003)

Recalling the occasion of the father
returning home to his two-year-old
daughter, after an absence of some
five days, a flood of heartwarming
emotions is the first overwhelming
sensation that seizes the stage in the
retelling. It's a feeling that stays
strong through the end, just as well.
First, though, it's also important to
note the quality of their communiques
during the trip; many very funny
Flash email cards from Hallmark made
the journey through the Internet to
reach from Boone to Hollywood, and
they were quite touching and
sentimental. "Miss Kiss" is one that
remains embedded in Amelia's mind,
about the time when her Daddy was in
California, when each was very sad.
Well, the phone conversations also
ran to new lengths and nuances . . .
giving both a chance to express
the love both had become so adept at
expressing through touch. Just as
is the case for anyone, the voice
on the phone can be a source for

painful feelings of things missing,
like sight and touch. This was the
most poignant instant yet in the
daughter's perception of "missing
Daddy," and the Daddy's, too. So,
by the time the date arose and the
daddy closed in on his return home,
anticipation was extraordinarily
high. He arrived, and he looked in
at his sleeping daughter in her
bedroom, and he and his beloved wife
seized the moment to lie down, rest
and catch-up together. Somehow, the
now-accustomed lonesomeness for each
other had added a new dimension,
which seemed to capture most of the
gravity in itself: their daughter.
The parents were joyful and focused
on ending the pain of parting that
they'd all suffered together, each
in their individual way. So, as
soon as an acceptable amount of nap
time had transpired, the father
climbed into bed with the little one,
and upon her waking up, he met the
sweetest words he could never even
imagine: in her whisper, she told
him, "I missed you." One little hand
on each of his cheeks, her smile said

the pain was gone, and he kissed her,
until he had to bury his face against
her chest and give in to the utter
sobs—quiet, happy ones—that rose
to the surface of his emotions. She
heard Daddy laugh, "Happy tears Baby!"

· · ·

#34 (NOV. 12, 2005)

So, let's discuss this 'writer' in more detail.
Fastidious, he'll have to be for sure, to make
progress in creating something brilliant
enough to ford his fate to any new height.
First things first, though, as he knows.
There's a story to be told. It must be
crafted superbly. Its language must be
inviting, captivating . . . calculating. Spot on.
That's what's missing—the ability to step
into the zone, where the mind can focus
completely on artistically rendering a tale
with depth, heart, soul, and stirrings of
ancient orders for living human spirits.
My goodness . . . it's no wonder I've decided
in the past to build up to this. It's quite the
pedestal I've parked my expectations on.
Whatever writing I take on, there are
rewards to be had, but creating content
I can own is what I'm driven to accomplish.
That seems something profound to savor.

So, there's a story to be crafted, as described. Making headway on that will be a respectable challenge in and of itself. Organizationally, strategically, I'm proud to say that I'm starting to gain traction. And I've done my share of long-form writing projects in the past. If I'm lucky, my future will have more big projects than are now in my past. And all will soar.

$$\cdot\ \cdot\ \cdot$$

#32 (FEB. 1, 2006)

Relating to my children is becoming more and more important to me. When I hold either of them, I realize how very much I love them. The physical connections between us remind me that I have made a person, who is now growing up. As they fare in the world, so do I, in every sense of the word. The life that spread itself over 36 years is now off the charts, quite literally. Our mental range is now restricted to the swift currents of the past 53 months, since the responsibility that came home with our first baby settled in. The dedication required to fulfill parental obligations is exactly what my wife and I were set to provide, at that point in life. We took a risk, struggled at first, and then

hit a stride like we never thought possible.
By the time we get through our next CPA
meeting, I expect to have a distinct plan
in hand for our financial future, including
early retirement, at least by a couple years.
The routine is rewarding us with security,
and it makes me very enthusiastic about
the world my children live in. And yet, the
days of our lives bring us grief, despair,
disaster, destruction . . . and cancer. These
Darnell children, so important and special;
how much security can I truly offer them?
My apprehension can never be fully offset,
but when we hold each other and know
that all is well, today, we are living large.

· · ·

#24 (MARCH 13, 2007)

An attempted ode on the beginning of life.
These days, the agenda involves sorting
powers of attorneys, wills for life and death,
guardians for children in the event both
parents die, separate trustees of the estate,
and of course backups for those named as
heirs to each station, plus their backups.
I have seen ends of lives—they're not pretty.
No one ever seems prepared. But in time,
looking back, it sort of looks like each was,
as the last of their waves eventually receded.

Even the pyramids will return to sand in time!
My little insurance gift, or my little empire
of feats, finances, and—pardon the popular
British expression—fuck-all (as it will no
doubt all turn out to be), may not amount
to a hill of beans in the grand scheme, but
I hope it will be a real blessing to my family.
They are the joy and devotion of my life, and
the best times I've passed here have been
the spans I've spent in warm happiness,
laughter, and even attending life's sorrows,
with them. Life offers more joy, with Roger
or not, with you or not, as it will always be.

. . .

#20 (DEC. 8, 2007)

A journey. A commitment. An idea.
An inspiration.
An experiment. A reward. A victory.
A therapy. A relief. A confession.
An approach. A monument. A cry.
A lament. An admission. An outreach.
A shame. An act. A gesture. A display.
An indiscretion. A performance.
An elixir. An epiphany. An enigma.
A catalyst. A catharsis. A transformation.
To discover. To dedicate. To evolve.
To relish.
To learn. To reach. To will.

To fathom. To expect. To purge.
To try. To excel. To blossom.
To listen. To understand. To accept.
To observe. To absolve. To interpret.
To relate. To channel.
To absorb. To celebrate. To comprehend.

• • •

#11 (NOV. 28, 2008)

tonight I watched the pieces fall into place
the words used to describe my own values
either to someone else or myself, either in
reality or some hoped-for future, all these
observations and ruminations on the most
important building ingredients I weigh
were united and elegantly whirled together
as my life's journey-to-date was laid bare,
and what I saw was that it added me all up
as this guy on the planet who has lived.
and from now on, I can add new material.

• • •

#5 (MARCH 24, 2011)

Tonight, I am very thankful to be a son,
a grandson, a brother, a nephew,
a cousin, a friend, a husband, and a dad.
Also, I'm grateful that my kids have much
to be thankful for, and they both know it.

15

Being

First published: October 1, 2011

*According to Eckhart Tolle, **BEING** is exclusively something we <u>feel</u>.*

L **IKE YOU** and everyone else of course, when it comes down to essential facts, I have my parents to thank for my existence. Following on through with my countdown 'Ramble' project, I end (for now) this shared journey. These words complete a poetic arc for yours truly, and looking ahead, I am aiming to write and produce new works you will find to be flat-out fascinating.

At this point in my life, I have grown to love the act of writing a poem. It's most sacred to me . . . and I tend to place so much value in words written during sustained periods of deep concerted thought that often just *being* is less satisfying than it is to read and write poetry, with an open mind that's ready, willing, and able to learn, think, and create. My passions for fine art, music, cinema, photography, design, and even architecture relate to my love for writing poems . . . but they are different, too, since poems rely on word-forms alone, which must speak out from otherwise blank pages. Where a few words can fill a space and fundamentally alter experiences, I am all-in, and extremely interested. To me, that is art at a very exciting level of creation and possibility.

It really makes me feel good to finish Ramble, and to share its final stanzas with you. The project has been counting down to these very seconds for over nine years . . . beginning with longish entries and following with shorter and shorter ones. As you will see, I am proud to present numbers 6 in homage to our son, 4 dedicated to my Dad, 3 for my Mom, and 2 for my exquisite wife.

The very last part is the single line that has intrigued me to no end throughout the life of this project. From the very beginning, I have wondered what I would write as the simple last line of my self-focused creative writing project, which by the way, I have written during an amazingly prolific and pivotal span as a bona fide grownup.

Can you understand why I will not be publishing Ramble #1 anywhere? I do have a first draft of it, but I intend to continue rewriting it for the rest of my days. For now, it's tucked away, awaiting fate and most likely, my further attempts at perfection. For holding it out, I sincerely beg your pardon, and invite you to savor these other short polished gemstones, reflecting—along with the other latest Rambles—

what I hold dearest. It has been a real honor to write and share this adventure with you. I like to imagine that you will have learned something worth knowing by taking up these tales with me, so I'll continue doing so, if you don't mind. If you do have any feedback to share, please don't be a stranger.

#6 (AUG. 18, 2010)

Riley has been for six and a half years,
and he is amazing, as it's widely known.
A great and true friend, little brother,
cousin, grandson, nephew, and son, we are
all cast in his rollicking adventure.
Wishes: Happy days, and smooth sailing.

• • •

#4 (MARCH 24, 2011)

My beloved father has always been my
supercharged intellectual model for myself
as business success, personality, and
family provider. The stuff of legend, JKD.

• • •

#3 (SEP. 28, 2011)

Perfect mother, you are my good fortune.
As you've led, I've followed to happiness.
Dream on and live in joy one most loved!

• • •

#2 (SEP. 28, 2011)

Beth: For all that you are, I am endlessly in awe and in love; and I'll always be.

. . .

ABOUT THE AUTHOR

Author, communications consultant, publisher, and career guide Roger Darnell is the principal of the Darnell Works Agency (DWA), the go-to PR firm for creative agencies, brands, and entertainment ventures. Since launching in 2000, the agency's clients have succeeded brilliantly, scoring top industry accolades, and collaborating with world-leading creative marketers to continually redefine cutting-edge creativity. Collectively, their projects have spanned original feature, short, and brand films, TV series, music videos, film and TV main titles and idents, top-rated Super Bowl spots, iconic network promos for major networks, and even Olympics openers.

A widely published author with global business contacts and numerous credits on independent feature films and network TV series, Roger is also the creator of the original travelogue series, "Rare Air." Certified as a U.S. Air Force Training Systems Specialist and winner of a Scripps-Howard Foundation fellowship for creative writing, he is especially drawn to filmmakers and studios. Through his partnership, his clients have secured festival screenings, distribution deals, panel appearances and keynote speaking engagements at prominent business and creative-industry conferences worldwide.

Supporting authors and artists, Roger has published and promoted many original books, custom publications, and art collections. In line with his values, he regularly contributes to non-profits aimed at protecting the environment and endangered species and helping homeless and other at-risk individuals. Married to Beth Darnell since 1992, and father to Amelia and Riley, Roger also takes immense pride in each of the recommendations he has received from clients and colleagues on LinkedIn, and in his friendships with some of the planet's coolest people.

www.rkdarnell.com

ACKNOWLEDGMENTS

As indicated, each chapter of this book has been published on the author's personal blog at **https://onup.darnellworks.com** since the date provided. "Ethereal Stones" appeared in the November, 1994, issue of Midwest Poetry Review, thanks to then-editor Tom Tilford. "John Wayne Dies Again" was published in the Summer 1995 issue of 24-7 Artzine.

The excerpt from "Four Quartets" by T.S. Eliot is published under license from Faber and Faber, Ltd.

Sam Hamill's "A Poet's Work: The Other Side of Poetry" has been reproduced with permission from Mr. Hamill's estate.

Thanks so much for reading!
If possible to add a rating and a short review on Amazon,
Goodreads, or to share your feedback by any other means,
it will be greatly appreciated
(especially if it's positive).

By visiting **rkdarnell.com**, you can also easily subscribe to the author's mailing list for game-changing insights, exclusives, extras, and giveaways. In the words of Craig Duncan, "Our time here is short, make the most of it!!!"